THE LAST LESSONS OF CHRIST

Living by Faith in an Age of Despair

Daniel Sweet and Andrew Gilmore

© 2019 Daniel Sweet and Andrew Gilmore
The Last Lessons of Christ: Living by Faith in an Age of Despair
First Edition, April 2019

Norman, OK
Sequoyah Trails Press

Content Editing: Kendall Davis, Kendall-Ashley.com
Copyediting: Shayla Raquel, ShaylaRaquel.com
Cover Design: Adam Haynes
Interior Formatting: Polgarus Studio, PolgarusStudio.com

The Last Lessons of Christ: Living by Faith in an Age of Despair is under copyright protection. No part of this book may be used or reproduced in any manner whatsoever without written permission except in the case of brief quotations embodied in critical articles and reviews. Printed in the United States of America. All rights reserved.

Unless otherwise noted, all Scripture quotations are from the ESV® Bible (The Holy Bible, English Standard Version®), copyright © 2001 by Crossway, a publishing ministry of Good News Publishers. Used by permission. All rights reserved.

Scripture quotations marked (NIV) are taken from the Holy Bible, New International Version®, NIV®. Copyright © 1973, 1978, 1984, 2011 by Biblica, Inc.™ Used by permission of Zondervan. All rights reserved worldwide. www.zondervan.com. The "NIV" and "New International Version" are trademarks registered in the United States Patent and Trademark Office by Biblica, Inc.™

ISBN 978-0-578-44494-9

Yours for free!
Explore every one of Christ's parables in this quick reference guide.

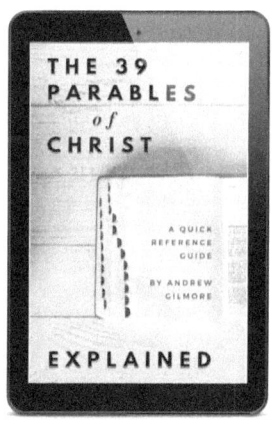

We've put together an extra resource as a way to say thank you for picking up this book. In this gift, you'll find a quick reference guide to all 39 of Jesus's parables in chronological order.

While the book you're about to read only contains the last few lessons Jesus taught his disciples, *The 39 Parables of Christ, Explained* contains every parable recorded in Scripture.

Download this guide, and you'll be able to quickly identify and locate any of Jesus's parables. In addition, each lesson has a brief summary and explanation. We think you'll really love it!

Visit bit.ly/39Parables to grab your free copy.

Contents

Preface vii

INTRODUCTION: When Darkness Seems to Be Winning 1

LESSON 1: Genuine Faith Defeats Darkness 13

LESSON 2: Jesus Will Return to End the Darkness . . .
So Get Busy 27

LESSON 3: Persist through the Darkness 39

LESSON 4: Religion Is Not the Solution 49

LESSON 5: Stop Working for Something You Cannot Earn 65

LESSON 6: Abandon Everything to Follow Jesus 79

LESSON 7: Faith Leads to Extraordinary Outcomes 95

LESSON 8: The Gospel Overcomes Darkness 109

LESSON 9: Faith Always Produces Action 125

LESSON 10: Jesus's Death Destroys Darkness 143

Acknowledgments 161
About the Authors 163
Connect with the Authors 165

Preface

The life of Jesus still fascinates me even though I've been following him since I was a teenager. As I continue to teach, preach, and study the Gospels, there are layers of depth that challenge our thinking, convict our actions, and move us into transformation. When I began an in-depth study into the ascension discourse, I was blown away by the idea that Jesus's last lessons to his disciples all seemed to center on faith. Jesus knew the disciples' faith would be critical in his absence. Today, followers of Jesus span the globe, and faith is more important than ever.

I look at today's culture and all around I see a strange sort of angst and anxiety. From a desperate outlook on the future from a younger generation to a pessimistic perspective from the older crowd, no one seems to think that the future can be bright. Perhaps it's because of political division and moral confusion; either way, there seems to be a fog of fatalism that has beset our culture and even infiltrated the church. So for this reason, I see Jesus's last lessons as incredibly important material each believer should consider.

I'm convinced that the missing ingredient in so many Christians' lives is the vibrant faith the rabbi challenged his disciples with as he marched toward Jerusalem. The church is the hope of the nations, and Christian people, including myself, must choose faith over fear every single day. In doing so, we will see the Lord break chains, move barriers, and transform our neighbors and nations!

Daniel Sweet

When Daniel approached me several years ago with his idea for a book, I was knee-deep in other writing projects. I had just wrapped up my second book a few months earlier, so I was focused on marketing it as best as I knew how. In addition, I had an idea for a new book I was (and still am) excited about. Because of these ventures, the temptation to say, "No thanks!" to Daniel's book proposal rested squarely on the tip of my tongue.

Yet, as I listened to my pastor pour out this seed of an idea he had, I could sense the passion and urgency in his voice. He saw a common thread among lessons Luke recorded in his gospel. Though these lessons seem disparate, they all revolve around one thing: a powerful, effective, world-changing faith. Contrast these lessons to the helplessness and hopelessness we see so often today, even among Christians, and well, the book basically wrote itself.

If only it were that easy. This project has been years in the making and one of the most laborious things I've ever done. But at the same time, the process has served to increase my own faith and give me a greater understanding of Jesus's mission while on earth. Our hope is that this book will do the same for you.

Andrew Gilmore

INTRODUCTION
When Darkness Seems to Be Winning

Men can be masters of their fate. It is not destiny's fault, but our own faults, that we're slaves.
—*Julius Caesar*, Shakespeare

Fate fascinates us. It teases our imaginations. Whether on the silver screen in romantic comedies and time travel flicks, or on the page in young adult novels, we see fate and destiny played out at every turn. The idea that a power beyond ourselves orders the course of events in our lives brings comfort to many and intrigue to many more. But these ideas aren't limited to the realm of fiction. A recent study by two Yale researchers revealed that among theists, nearly 85 percent of those surveyed believe in some measure of fate.[1] You might expect such a response from those who believe in a god, but even a majority of atheists—54 percent—confessed a belief in fate. And if that weren't enough, consider this staggering Gallup survey from the turn of the twenty-first century. When asked if they believed in astrology—defined as the belief that the position of the planets or stars can affect people's lives—25 percent of respondents in the US

---

[1] Kelsey Dallas, "When It Comes to Fate, Even Non-Believers Believe," *Deseret News*, December 5, 2014, https://www.deseretnews.com/article/865617028/Study-Believers-and-atheists-alike-believe-everything-happens-for-a-reason.html.

and Canada responded in the affirmative.[2]

In a post-enlightenment culture, why are we so enamored with fate? The reasons are many. The most obvious is that reason alone cannot account for everything in life, especially the experiential. How can a scientist account for sacrificial love, the perception of beauty, human consciousness, or the origin of the universe? No amount of scientific scholarship can explain these mysteries. Another factor is the comfort destiny provides in its explanatory power. *Everything happens for a reason. It just wasn't meant to be.* We toss out these clichés as reminders that we aren't in control of our own lives.

One could also point to the influence of Hollywood on pop culture. Of course, not every movie ends with good triumphing over evil, with love finding a way, and with life lived happily ever after, but even in dark films, the typical viewer is not satisfied without some type of resolution in the end. Yet another factor might be the influx of Eastern and New Age mysticism to the West.

Certainly the Bible teaches that God is all powerful and his will cannot be overcome. As Job said to the Almighty, "I know that you can do all things, and that no purpose of yours can be thwarted" (Job 42:2). Consider also this reminder from the proverb, "The heart of man plans his way, but the LORD establishes his steps" (Prov. 16:9). God is sovereign and can do what he wants, when he wants.

Yet I wonder about fate's claim on humanity. Are certain outcomes just meant to be? Are the events of our lives simply out of our control? Is fate at the helm of our lives?

---

[2] Linda Lyons, "Paranormal Beliefs Come (Super)Naturally to Some," *Gallup*, November 1, 2005, http://news.gallup.com/poll/19558/paranormal-beliefs-come-supernaturally-some.aspx.

Raiders at the Gate

I ask these questions from a pastor's perspective. A major problem lurks in churches, American culture, and even in my own community. Though it may suit the silver screen, in reality destiny has a dark side.

Fate seems wonderful when life is going well, but what about when everything goes wrong? When the protagonist doesn't get the girl? When you don't win the lottery? What happens when a white spot shows up on the Xray? Believing in fate when bad things happen flips our ordered lives upside down and inside out. A depressing and helpless mind-set descends upon us. There's a name for this. It's called *fatalism*—the belief that you can't effect change in the world or even in your own life. And even if you don't believe in fate, it's hard not to succumb to fatalism, believing and acting as though nothing you do really matters.

Why is it so hard to avoid fatalism?

Because darkness seems to be winning. There are proverbial raiders at the gate of our culture. Injustice, illness, and other forms of suffering appear to be smothering any hope we have of redemption. Since the ejection from Eden, humanity has been no stranger to brokenness—from the biblical flood to Nero, Hitler, and beyond. But today's ills seem more potent and prevalent than ever:

- Terrorism
- Human trafficking
- Racial prejudice and injustice
- The relegation of people of faith to the fringes of culture
- The rise of atheism, nihilism, and hedonism in an increasingly secular society
- Attacks on the biblical view of marriage
- Gender identity confusion

One contributing factor to this breakdown in our society, communities, churches, and even our everyday lives is the decline of the family unit. In the past, when moral decay and uncertainty raged within society, we had our homes as a place of refuge. A place where Mom, Dad, Sister, and Brother formed the foundation of stability in our little world. But today, homes are often the source of violence, and divorce is embraced as a normal part of culture. An increasing number of children grow up in single-parent homes. The once traditional nuclear family is now considered uncommon. In tandem, America aborts three thousand babies every day, politicizes marriage, and distorts beyond recognition God's design for sex. As a result, the foundation of society is crumbling and teetering on the edge of collapse.

Rather than stand strong against the shifting moral winds, many churches have untethered themselves from the gospel and embraced the world. When once the church was a moral compass, those who have relied on her find it harder every day to locate true north. Many churches have watered down the gospel, resulting in a biblically illiterate congregate. Is it any wonder that the masses are fleeing church? Despite the existence of numerous mega churches, fewer people attend religious services than ever before. Even in the most evangelized cities, the majority of the population claims no religious affiliation whatsoever. I minister in Norman, Oklahoma, a community on the southern edge of the Oklahoma City metro. Despite its residence in the Bible Belt, where the adage boasts "a church on every corner," nearly 60 percent of the population in my city has zero religious connection, Christian or otherwise.[3] So as anti-

---

[3] "County Membership Report: Cleveland County, Oklahoma, Religious Traditions, 2010," The Association of Religion Data Archives, http://www.thearda.com/rcms2010/r/c/40/rcms2010_40027_county_name_2010.asp.

God thinking continues its assault on traditional values, dwindling attendance forces church after church to close its doors.

This is not meant to depress you, but rather to expose one root of fatalism. And when this mind-set invades our thinking, negativity, disheartening headlines, and violence cause us to despair because we can't see a way out of it all. So we close ourselves off and grow numb to moral decay and social unrest. As my friend and philosophy professor Dr. Kuhn said, "Things seem to be changing so fast that many are feeling a real existential angst and helplessness to do anything about it." Whatever you call it, a fatalistic viewpoint is a serious problem. It is one thing for the non-believing community to accept it as a worldview. However, when the church begins swallowing the poison of fatalism, her collapse becomes inevitable. Let me be clear: Christ's church cannot fail (Matt. 16:18). She is the hope of nations and Jesus's hands and feet on earth. But the ineffective faith resulting from fatalistic thought renders individual churches weak and useless.

Yet some would argue that today's reality has unfolded exactly the way it is supposed to. Some may even argue that, like a Greek tragedy, no one can do anything about all of the terrible things happening in our country and communities. Seriously, what can any one person do about the collapse of Judeo-Christian values in America? Should we just accept the fact that we live in a post-Christian culture? Maybe all of this was supposed to happen this way.

These statements do well to articulate fatalism, but the dictionary is instructive too. Webster defines *fatalism* as the belief that "what will happen has already been decided and cannot be changed."[4] This is helplessness to its core, and while the overwhelming presence of evil is one source, another force is also a partner.

---

[4] "Fatalism," *Merriam-Webster.com*, http://www.merriam-webster.com/dictionary/fatalism.

Dawkins, Harris, and Affluenza

New atheism is all the craze. Atheism is nothing new, but its most recent sect has become militant and almost evangelical. No longer are secular humanists satisfied to allow the religious folk to continue about their "misguided" way. New atheism seeks to destroy, discredit, and embarrass anything that betrays a naturalistic worldview. Evolutionary biologist Richard Dawkins is the forerunner of this movement, and his worldview is picking up momentum. Like all atheists, he thinks nothing exists beyond the natural world. In addition, he also believes all forms of religion, particularly Christianity, are a threat to human progress and should be stopped. He and others who believe like him seek to convert people to atheism and encourage them to join their secular crusade. Without question, an important feature of atheism—increasing in popularity thanks to the new atheists—is fatalism.

Perhaps one of the more concerning features of atheism is its position regarding ethics and morality. Whether atheists admit it or not, a naturalistic worldview requires deterministic ethics. In other words, if people are nothing but highly evolved animals, comprised of nothing but chemicals and matter, then the way a man or woman behaves is entirely out of his or her control. Still not convinced? Dawkins said, "DNA neither cares nor knows; DNA just is. And we dance to its music."[5] In other words, we humans are just an accidental product of evolution, and our genetic programming is driving every action we take. In the words of Carl Sagan, we are "star stuff." Naturalistic, mechanical accidents. Therefore, people do whatever they do because they are supposed to do it. Like a lion on the Serengeti, we are simply living out our biological impulses and responding to stimuli.

---

[5] Richard Dawkins, *River Out of Eden: A Darwinian View of Life* (New York: Basic Books, 2004), 133.

You may be thinking, "That's silly. I have free will." Not so according to another famous atheist and neuroscientist Sam Harris. In his book, *Free Will*, Harris argues that human freedom is an illusion. People are who they are and do what they do because of genetics and conditioning, nothing more. While it may seem like humans have a choice in the things they do and the people they become, that freedom is an illusion. A façade. That's comforting, isn't it? Such a worldview leaves us with a moral system in which people cannot be held accountable for their actions—no more than a lion can be held accountable for forcibly copulating with a lioness.

As an example, consider the chilling story of sixteen-year-old Ethan Couch. In the summer of 2013, Couch crashed his pickup truck into four people who were changing a tire on the side of a Texas road. All four were killed. At the time of the accident, Ethan's blood alcohol content was almost three times the legal limit. But instead of receiving jail time, a juvenile court judge sentenced the teen to just ten months of substance abuse therapy.[6] What was Couch's defense? How did he get off? He claimed affluenza. Apparently, affluenza is a condition in which a young person is so spoiled by his parents that he cannot be held accountable for his actions. The affected suffers from being too affluent! This young man's defense argued that because Ethan's parents gave him everything he wanted and never bothered disciplining their son, *they* were actually responsible for the crime.

You heard that right. According to the judge, Ethan Couch couldn't help but drink while underage and then get behind the wheel. (Never mind that he and his friends had stolen the very

---

[6] Dana Ford, "Texas Teen Ethan Couch Gets 10 Years' Probation for Driving Drunk, Killing 4," *Cable News Network*, December 12, 2013, http://www.cnn.com/2013/12/11/us/texas-teen-dwi-wreck/.

alcohol that filled his veins the night of the accident.[7]) And it wasn't Ethan's fault he was driving seventy miles per hour on a two-lane road where the speed limit is only forty. It wasn't his fault he plowed through good Samaritans who were helping a stranded young woman change a tire. Apparently, Ethan is just a mechanical organism capable of responding accordingly to stimuli and conditions that are out of his control. Apparently, he cannot really make decisions at all. What happened that night was fate—naturalism at work. It was just meant to be. Who are we to hold this poor kid accountable?

Get the picture?

For those outside of the body of Christ, fatalism seems to be the only viable mind-set amid such chaos; young Ethan was simply acting out his programming based on his environment. But too many churches have also allowed this deterministic thinking to infiltrate their pews, pulpits, and ministries. Why is this? Again, many Christians are simply overwhelmed by the evil in the world and therefore feel like nothing they do can effect change. For others, fate brings comfort because it relieves them of their responsibility to act. If everything is predetermined, then what good would it do to serve others? Why should one care for orphans and widows? God's got this. *If he wants me to serve, he'll make me do it.* Yet another reason is bad theology. Some churches teach fatalism as a core belief. They don't call it that, but the logical outworking of their doctrine leads straight to despair.

No matter how one arrives at fatalism, the mentality is ungodly for the Christ follower. How do I know? Jesus taught something radically different.

---

[7] Ibid.

Walking with Jesus

Believe it or not, Jesus addressed this very question in a series of parables, miracles, and object lessons directed at his disciples. Just prior to Passion Week, the Lord's final week on earth, Jesus traveled on foot from Capernaum in northern Galilee to Jerusalem. This trip would typically take five to six days, and due to the uneven terrain of Israel would require some zigzagging around mountains. First, the group would head south toward Samaria before turning east to cross the Jordan River. It was not uncommon to continue south through Samaria—doing so shaved off a full day of travel time[8]—but the ultra-religious avoided the territory if at all possible. Jews and Samaritans did not get along, and the Pharisees preferred to bypass the region altogether.[9] In addition, taking this direct route through Samaria, although shorter, yielded more treacherous terrain. Jesus, it appears, had planned to use the Samaria route, but the Samaritans rejected him because he had his eyes set on Jerusalem.[10] So instead, they headed east to the Jordan River Valley. After crossing the river, they would travel due south through the valley until almost reaching the Dead Sea. At that point, they would turn back west, crossing the river again toward Jericho and then continuing through Jericho to Jerusalem where Jesus would enter riding a donkey and be greeted by hosannas and palm branches. A week later, he would be dead.

What's interesting is that as Passion Week looms, and Jesus gets ever closer to Jerusalem, Luke includes multiple accounts related to

---

[8] Traveling straight through Samaria shortened the trip by twenty-three miles, about a day's journey. See Merilyn Hargis, "On the Road," *Christianity Today*, http://www.christianitytoday.com/history/issues/issue-59/on-road.html.
[9] Charles Ellicott, "John 4: Ellicott's Commentary for English Readers," *Bible Hub*, http://biblehub.com/commentaries/ellicott/john/4.htm.
[10] See Luke 9:51–56.

faith. Jesus seems obsessed with the subject. Why? His ministry is coming to a close and his death is imminent. Soon, the kingdom would be in the hands of his ragtag group of disciples. Jesus knew his followers would soon face persecution, and they would need resilient faith to persist through such adversity. Their journey from Capernaum to Jerusalem was the last opportunity Jesus would have on earth to instill in his disciples whatever wisdom or instruction they would need. These were the last lessons of Christ, and they almost exclusively centered on faith.

In some ways, the disciples' time with Jesus was practice for the mammoth task of carrying the message of Christ to the nations. He sent them out in twos as training for ministry. When they messed up, the Lord was there to correct them. Post-resurrection, it would be the disciples' duty to move the kingdom of heaven forward on earth, and they would have to do so without Jesus present.

Certainly, Jesus had been teaching the disciples about faith all through his earthly ministry. Consider previous miracles like feeding the five thousand when he commanded his disciples, "You give them something to eat" (Luke 9:13). The Twelve were flabbergasted at this statement, insisting such a task was impossible. But Jesus demonstrated that with faith, feeding the crowd was indeed possible. In addition to miracles, Jesus told parables about faith like the analogy of the mustard seed. The smallest of seeds, he said, yields the largest of trees, just as a small amount of faith can lead to enormous results. Without a doubt, Jesus taught the disciples about faith for the duration of his three-year ministry. However, these last few moments before the triumphal entry were critical teaching moments Jesus used to help solidify their trust in their Lord before the storm of the crucifixion set in.

In stark contrast to helplessness and hopelessness, Jesus taught his disciples about the importance of faith. Too many of us, whipped by the world, have reduced faith to a passive belief in something beyond ourselves. But Jesus taught a faith with power and agency, faith that can move mountains. We submit that things can change and that we can change them. We believe your faith matters.

With this book, through the filter of these last lessons of Jesus, we intend to cast a new light on societal ills so that when faced with them, you will feel hope rather than resignation. That in the face of destruction and brokenness, you will see opportunities for advancing God's kingdom rather than the powerlessness the world and even some theological approaches might leave you with. We'll begin in Luke 17 and travel with Jesus and his crew, following them until just prior to his triumphal entry in Jerusalem in chapter 19. When we pick up with Jesus, he is somewhere between Galilee and Samaria[11]— near the beginning of his trip. We'll see parables, object lessons, and miracles from which we can glean truths related to living out a vibrant faith even in the face of brokenness.

So how would you live your life if you truly believed you could effect change? If you bought into the reality that the universe is not controlled by fate? That your actions, your decisions, your beliefs, and your faith *do* make a difference? What if I told you that you can be an instrument of change, a person who helps push back darkness and defeats evil?

The final chapter of Revelation has already been written, and Jesus will return to judge the living and the dead. But what happens between now and Christ's return is not written. Does God know what's going to transpire? Of course he does, but foreknowledge does not equal causation. As with so many people in the Scriptures— Noah, Abraham, Moses, Joseph, Esther, Mary, and many more— God wants to use you to effect positive change for the kingdom. He

---

[11] See Luke 17:11.

can do it without you, but he'd rather have you on board. Just as Jesus concerned himself with building up the faith of his disciples, he also cares deeply about the development of your faith. God wants to use you to build his kingdom, but to be his instrument, it will require one thing above all: faith.

LESSON 1
Genuine Faith Defeats Darkness

Above all the grace and the gifts that Christ gives to his beloved is that of overcoming self.
—St. Francis of Assisi

The Sacred Text

"Pay attention to yourselves! If your brother sins, rebuke him, and if he repents, forgive him, and if he sins against you seven times in the day, and turns to you seven times, saying, 'I repent,' you must forgive him."

The apostles said to the Lord, "Increase our faith!" And the Lord said, "If you had faith like a grain of mustard seed, you could say to this mulberry tree, 'Be uprooted and planted in the sea,' and it would obey you.

"Will any one of you who has a servant plowing or keeping sheep say to him when he has come in from the field, 'Come at once and recline at table'? Will he not rather say to him, 'Prepare supper for me, and dress properly, and serve me while I eat and drink, and afterward you will eat and drink'? Does he thank the servant because he did what was commanded? So you also, when you have done all that you were commanded, say, 'We are unworthy servants; we have only done what was our duty.'"

On the way to Jerusalem he was passing along between

Samaria and Galilee. And as he entered a village, he was met by ten lepers, who stood at a distance and lifted up their voices, saying, "Jesus, Master, have mercy on us." When he saw them he said to them, "Go and show yourselves to the priests." And as they went they were cleansed. Then one of them, when he saw that he was healed, turned back, praising God with a loud voice; and he fell on his face at Jesus' feet, giving him thanks. Now he was a Samaritan. Then Jesus answered, "Were not ten cleansed? Where are the nine? Was no one found to return and give praise to God except this foreigner?" And he said to him, "Rise and go your way; your faith has made you well."

—Luke 17:3–19

As we pick up with Jesus on his journey, he's about to give three lessons which teach that pride and selfishness are antidotes to effective faith. Any attempt at making a difference for the kingdom must begin with a foundation of selflessness. As Jesus taught, these three essential qualities are forgiveness, service, and gratitude. The first episode comes at the beginning of Luke 17. As Christ inched nearer to Jerusalem, Jesus reminded Peter, John, and the gang that when a person sins against them, they should offer forgiveness many times over:

> If your brother sins, rebuke him, and if he repents, forgive him, and if he sins against you seven times in the day, and turns to you seven times, saying, "I repent," you must forgive him.
> —Luke 17:3–4

Has anyone ever wronged you? I'm willing to bet someone has. Could you imagine someone doing the same offensive thing to you *seven* times in one day? That's the hyperbolic scenario Jesus painted.

I (Daniel) had a neighbor once whose dog continually nosed his way into my trash. It almost never failed that after I hauled my dumpster out the night before trash day, the next morning I would wake up to refuse scattered throughout my yard. The perpetrator was always the same dog from three houses down. But solving the crime does no good if no one does anything about the criminal. My neighbor made no attempt to keep the dog in his yard and never helped pick up the dirty diapers and old pizza boxes. So begrudgingly, I would get up each Thursday morning to pick up trash, all the while reminding myself to love my neighbor. As frustrating as this scenario was, I had a whole week to forgive, cool off, and move on.

Can you imagine if this offense took place seven times in one day, and each time my neighbor begged for forgiveness? It seems ludicrous to have to forgive someone so often. That's why the disciples pleaded with Jesus, "Increase our faith!" What he taught them seemed impossible. But picking up trash is trivial compared to another example of forgiveness. In 2016, Oklahoma City Thunder assistant coach Monty Williams lost his wife in an automobile accident to a negligent driver. So when the coach claimed he harbored no ill will for the family of the woman who caused his wife's death, it was hard to take him at face value. The difficulty lay not in his body language or timing or facial expressions—classically trained actors couldn't have given a more genuine delivery. Instead, the incredulity arose from the circumstances surrounding the statement.

On February 9, 2016, Ingrid Williams was driving north on South Western Avenue with three of her five kids when a woman in a Chevrolet Impala approached traveling a blistering ninety-two miles per hour in a zone limited to forty. The woman, Susannah Donaldson, clipped another vehicle, causing her to lose control of her own car and swerve into oncoming traffic. Her vehicle struck Ingrid's Suburban head-on, killing Donaldson instantly. Ingrid would die soon after.

If speeding were Ms. Donaldson's only error, perhaps Monty's peace offering to the Donaldsons would not have been so unbelievable. But in addition to driving at fastball speed, police reported Susannah appeared to have been driving with her dog in her lap, no doubt contributing to the driver's overall distractedness.[12] And if imprudence with canines and reckless speeds weren't enough, the real kicker came when officials ran the toxicology report. Ms. Donaldson tested positive for methamphetamine and amphetamine.[13]

So when Monty stood up at Crossings Community Church in Oklahoma City to honor the life of his late wife and mother of his five young children, the last thing anyone expected was compassion for the family of the drugged-up driver who caused an otherwise avoidable collision. But that's exactly what happened:

> Everybody's praying for me and my family, which is right. But let us not forget that there were two people in this situation. And that family needs prayer as well. And we have no ill will towards that family. In my house we have a sign that says, "As for me and my house we will serve the Lord." We cannot serve the Lord if we don't have a heart of forgiveness.

---

[12] Jonathan Greco, "Police Release Information on Crash That Killed Wife of Thunder Assistant Coach," *KOCO News 5*, February 11, 2016, http://www.koco.com/article/police-release-information-on-crash-that-killed-wife-of-thunder-assistant-coach/4308267.

[13] Jonathan Greco, "Driver in Accident That Killed Ingrid Williams Tested Positive for Meth," *KOCO News 5*, March 25, 2016, http://www.koco.com/article/driver-in-accident-that-killed-ingrid-williams-tested-positive-for-meth/4309061.

That family didn't wake up wanting to hurt my wife. Life is hard. It is very hard. And that was tough, but we hold no ill will towards the Donaldson family, and we as a group, brothers united in unity, should be praying for that family because they grieve as well. So let's not lose sight of what's important.[14]

What's important? What was he talking about? What could possibly be more important in that moment than grieving over the loss of Ingrid, Monty's soul mate? With an unnatural, perhaps supernatural, dose of wisdom, Monty transcended the moment and the circumstances to focus on the eternal aspects of the situation. There's more theology in those few sentences than in many sermons you'll hear. *Pray for your enemies. Do unto others as you would have them do unto you. Forgive your brother and sister. Remove the plank from your own eye. Love covers a multitude of sins.*

Monty's children, who survived the accident, were in the audience for that eulogy, and he wanted them to hear the words of forgiveness. He understood that that moment was about more than just himself and his pain. As he said, "My wife would punch me if I were to sit up here and whine about what's going on." The tragedy he had experienced gave him a platform for testifying to God's goodness and grace. And when faced with a hideous situation, Monty did what Ingrid would have wanted him to do: he forgave the woman who caused her death. Unbelievable.

---

[14] "NBA's Monty Williams Urges 'Heart of Forgiveness' at Wife's Funeral," YouTube video, 4:45, posted by "The Christian Broadcasting Network," February 19, 2016, https://youtu.be/Q2vrZPbQ9r4?t=4m45s.

Absorbing Evil

I tell this story only to illustrate that your attitude is the driving force for kingdom-centric living. You must develop a sacrificial, selfless disposition to make an impact on the world. What happened to Mr. Williams was unfair, pointless, and totally avoidable. And yet, while he could have allowed himself to drown in his sorrow, anger, and loss, the basketball coach instead chose to use the opportunity for God's glory. Lest you think Monty Williams is some kind of Saint or superhero, listen to what else he had to say in that same eulogy:

> We can't lose sight of the fact that God loves us. And that's what my wife . . . and that's what I try to, however badly, exhibit on a daily basis. But God does love us. He loved me so much that he sent his son to die for my sins, and I for one know that I am not the man that you guys see every day. And only God could cover that.[15]

Do you see the incredible power the gospel has? When it could have been so tempting to focus on the sins of Susannah Donaldson, to lash out at the irresponsibility and idiocy of driving ninety-two miles per hour with a dog in your lap while high on meth, Williams instead brought up his own sin. He knew that impacting the world for Christ meant relinquishing pride.

No doubt all of us struggle at times with forgiveness, but Jesus wanted his followers to understand its importance. If you think about it, forgiveness is the basis for all of Christianity. God pardons sinful humans through the atoning work of the cross. We did not deserve the grace imparted to us, but the Father granted it nevertheless. Not only did Jesus teach forgiveness with words, he also backed up those

---

[15] Ibid., 1:22.

words through the cross. He absorbed our punishment, and even to his last breath, he prayed, "Father, forgive them, for they know not what they do" (Luke 23:34).

So when we are wronged by the world or even by fellow believers, and we offer forgiveness, we model the love of Christ to those around us. In forgiveness, we acknowledge that we have been forgiven of a multitude of sins as well, and we testify that we trust in God for justice and judgment. He is the righteous and perfect judge. Therefore, forgiveness stops the cycle of revenge and escalation because we leave justice in the hands of God. What Jesus taught his disciples here is that one of the most effective ways to beat evil is, in essence, to absorb it through forgiveness. This requires an immense amount of faith because it means trusting in God for justice. If you think that sounds difficult, it is. But try commanding a tree to go plant itself in the ocean. With even a tiny amount of faith, Jesus said both are possible.

Mercenary Christians

In our second episode, we find another key to effective faith: servitude. It's no coincidence Jesus followed his tough words on forgiveness with a parable about faithful service. To the disciples Jesus posed a series of rhetorical questions designed to lead them to a proper view of service. He said:

> Will any one of you who has a servant plowing or keeping sheep say to him when he has come in from the field, "Come at once and recline at table"? Will he not rather say to him, "Prepare supper for me, and dress properly, and serve me while I eat and drink, and afterward you will eat and drink"? Does he thank the servant because he did what

was commanded? So you also, when you have done all that you were commanded, say, "We are unworthy servants; we have only done what was our duty."
—Luke 17:7–10

Would a master wait on a servant? Does a servant get special recognition for simply doing his job? Of course not! Jesus taught that a servant is concerned, first and foremost, with the master's desires. That is the purpose of a servant after all: to perform his or her duty. But what does service have to do with faith, and how does it affect your daily life?

Consider two occupations: a mercenary and a volunteer soldier. Both perform nearly identical duties (e.g., fighting for a state or a kingdom). Both mercenaries and soldiers risk their lives. They both fight against the same enemy. But there is a critical difference between the two. A mercenary, though employed by a king or head of state, fights for himself. He's in it for the reward. When the battle is over, he expects payment and can then move on to the next fight without expressing allegiance to the kingdom. In fact, if the price is right, the mercenary might soon find himself fighting against the very king for which he once provided his services. The volunteer soldier, on the other hand, is sold out for the kingdom. He is invested in the nation. He is motivated not by money but by a desire to see the kingdom persist and thrive. Yes, if victorious, the soldier will likely receive spoils from war, but personal gain is not his primary motivation. His heart is in the battle, but the mercenary? He's in it for himself. If you found yourself in a war, with whom would you rather fight?

I wonder how many Christ followers operate their lives as mercenaries rather than soldiers. How many turned to Jesus only to escape hell? Mercenary Christians go to church as if it were jury duty.

They pay tithe as if it were a tax. When they serve, they make sure to clock in so that they can be reimbursed for their servitude when they meet God in heaven. Do you know any mercenary Christians? If you do, you'll know they are ineffective in their faith. Instead of serving wholeheartedly simply because God is God and they are humans, they do just enough to preserve their reward (or so the thinking goes). They treat their relationship with God like a contract.

But those who serve with pure motives will carry out God's will no matter the cost, even if there's no guarantee of recompense. They are willing to sacrifice time. They are willing to move to the third world or give up a big pay raise so they will have more time for ministry. Living with this attitude activates our faith by turning our focus outward. Rather than serving for personal gain, we serve for the advancement of the kingdom.

If you are a Christ follower, you are also, by definition, his servant. But to serve Christ, you must trust that he is good, worthy, and honorable. Otherwise, how can you ever be faithful? Fear may drive a servant to fulfill his or her duty for a time, but fear will never produce faithfulness like trust will. A servant's diligence requires commitment, devotion, and a great deal of faithfulness. Faithfulness, of course, requires faith—an unwavering trust in the unseen. Hebrews 11:1 defines faith as the certainty of things hoped for and assuredness of things that are unseen. You and I cannot see God, but we see evidence of him through his revelations, and through those revelations, we know he is good. In response, we willingly serve him, acting on that evidence. This type of faith—faith that moves us to committed service—is a requirement for advancing the kingdom on earth.

Beyond Wellness, beyond Salvation

Through the first two episodes, we saw the manifestation of faith in forgiveness (trusting that God is a righteous judge), and faith in servitude (trusting that God is good and therefore worthy of our service). In the third episode, we see the transformative power of faith expressed through gratitude.

As Jesus and his disciples continued their journey south to Jerusalem, Jesus's lectures paused in favor of an object lesson. Somewhere between Galilee and Samaria, the travelers encountered a small leper colony:

> On the way to Jerusalem he was passing along between Samaria and Galilee. And as he entered a village, he was met by ten lepers, who stood at a distance and lifted up their voices, saying, "Jesus, Master, have mercy on us." When he saw them he said to them, "Go and show yourselves to the priests." And as they went they were cleansed.
> —Luke 17:11–14

By law, those with leprosy had to stay quarantined, prohibited from approaching anyone. But aware of the Lord's abilities, ten lepers begged to be healed. Being loving, compassionate, and all-powerful, Jesus healed these ten men as they followed his instruction to go and present themselves to the priests. Because the lepers trusted Jesus, they did what he said. Understanding Jesus had the power to heal them, they had confidence that what they hoped for—a life free of disease—they would receive.

But the story doesn't end there. Jesus isn't concerned only with the body but much more with the condition of the soul. The real concern is placed on the one Samaritan leper who had enough faith to return and express his gratitude. Here's the rest of the story:

> Then one of them, when he saw that he was healed, turned back, praising God with a loud voice; and he fell on his face at Jesus' feet, giving him thanks. Now he was a Samaritan. Then Jesus answered, "Were not ten cleansed? Where are the nine? Was no one found to return and give praise to God except this foreigner?" And he said to him, "Rise and go your way; your faith has made you well."
> —Luke 17:15–19

"Your faith has made you well." Why would Jesus say this? Weren't all ten lepers healed? Just because they were cured of their physical condition does not mean they were "well." Certainly, the lives of all ten lepers were changed. No doubt about it. Leprosy is a nasty disease. But what was the lesson for the disciples? Faith can make a person well—not (necessarily) divine healing, but rather spiritual wellness. Christ's power healed ten lepers of their physical ailment, but this last man's healing was also spiritual because of his faith. He was the only one who had faith to return and express gratitude to the Lord. As a result, he experienced both physical and spiritual healing. He was born again! Now you might be wondering if the actions of the Samaritan were really an expression of faith. Does gratitude require faith?

Gratitude is an acknowledgment of God's goodness, but more than that, the Samaritan declared in returning that goodness is only possible because of God. This isn't just a man turning back to say thank you. The scripture tells us he praised God and fell at Jesus's feet. The other nine lepers, on the contrary, may have fallen into two categories we still see today. One crowd might take the humanist approach and believe that by their own effort, they were healed. They shouted down Jesus. They obeyed his command and started toward the priest. The other crowd is the entitlement folks. They believe that because of religious status, works, or heritage, they are entitled to good things from God. This is why Jesus highlights the fact that the man who returned to express gratitude was a Samaritan. The other nine, presumably Jewish, demonstrated a sense of entitlement to healing because they descended from Abraham and were included in the Old Covenant. The Samaritan, on the other hand, with his mixed heritage, did not assume he deserved physical healing and returned to Jesus to praise him. And in doing so, not only was he healed in body but also in spirit.

What an important lesson for the twelve disciples who saw this unfold. Remember Jesus is preparing the disciples for his absence. In a matter of days, they would be on their own, and hordes of people would come to them for physical healing, just like the lepers came to Christ. Jesus demonstrated care for the physical condition as a bridge to heal the spiritual illness inside all the unsaved. The disciples needed to see that faith is what brings spiritual wellness to a person's soul. In this case, gratitude was an expression of the Samaritan man's faith. He was convinced that Jesus was the Messiah. As a result, the man experienced radical transformation. Leading others to this type of spiritual metamorphosis is the ultimate goal of all disciples. It's more than salvation. Everything about this man was different. Where once he was an outcast, a foreigner, and suffering from disease, now he was restored physically and spiritually. This is the gospel played out before their eyes!

This story of healing is powerful because we can look at it from two perspectives—Jesus's point of view and the Samaritan's viewpoint when it comes to making a difference for God's kingdom. Just like Jesus demonstrated, you and I must concern ourselves with the physical suffering of mankind as a step to leading others to Christ. Jesus could have easily ignored the requests of the ten lepers for healing. Instead, he had compassion on them and cared for their bodily needs. Doing so led directly to the salvation of the Samaritan leper. We also must have the compassion of Christ. More specifically, we must allow God to use us in any and every way to bring people to a faith response.

From the Samaritan's perspective, we must also live lives of gratitude, which is an acknowledgment of God's goodness. Luke tells us the healed man praised God with a loud voice. He wasn't trying to be obnoxious. This isn't like the Pharisees' loud prayers for which they desired praise from men. The Samaritan man simply could not contain the joy and gratitude he felt in his heart. What other reaction could he have? Living with gratitude transforms us into generous people, and that generosity serves as a witness to the world. The more we give, the more we express the love of Christ to the world.

Though these lessons on forgiveness, service, and gratitude seem disparate, they share a common foundation. All three point to one thing: *selflessness*. Less of me and more of Jesus. Forgiveness stops the cycle of evil by absorbing it and relinquishing it to God. He is our judge, and justice belongs in his hands, not ours. That sentence is easy to write, but extremely difficult to live out. This is why the disciples cried out for Jesus to increase their faith. Duty causes one to serve without motivation of reward, and it transforms us from self-centered to servant-oriented. From mercenary to missionary. Last, a posture of gratitude acknowledges God's goodness and changes us into generous people. When you combine these three elements—forgiveness, service, and gratitude—you see a model of Christ that can change the world for the better. People who live with these three elements are those you see on the frontlines of natural disasters, in the soup kitchens, and at the altars on Sundays. Put simply: effective faith requires pure motivations.

LESSON 2
Jesus Will Return to End the Darkness... So Get Busy

When you arise in the morning, think of what a precious privilege it is to be alive—to breathe, to think, to enjoy, to love.
—Marcus Aurelius

The Sacred Text

Being asked by the Pharisees when the kingdom of God would come, he answered them, "The kingdom of God is not coming in ways that can be observed, nor will they say, 'Look, here it is!' or 'There!' for behold, the kingdom of God is in the midst of you."

And he said to the disciples, "The days are coming when you will desire to see one of the days of the Son of Man, and you will not see it. And they will say to you, 'Look, there!' or 'Look, here!' Do not go out or follow them. For as the lightning flashes and lights up the sky from one side to the other, so will the Son of Man be in his day. But first he must suffer many things and be rejected by this generation. Just as it was in the days of Noah, so will it be in the days of the Son of Man. They were eating and drinking and marrying and being given in marriage, until the day when Noah entered the ark, and the flood came and destroyed them all. Likewise, just as it was in the days of Lot—they were eating

and drinking, buying and selling, planting and building, but on the day when Lot went out from Sodom, fire and sulfur rained from heaven and destroyed them all—so will it be on the day when the Son of Man is revealed. On that day, let the one who is on the housetop, with his goods in the house, not come down to take them away, and likewise let the one who is in the field not turn back. Remember Lot's wife. Whoever seeks to preserve his life will lose it, but whoever loses his life will keep it. I tell you, in that night there will be two in one bed. One will be taken and the other left. There will be two women grinding together. One will be taken and the other left." And they said to him, "Where, Lord?" He said to them, "Where the corpse is, there the vultures will gather."
—Luke 17:20–37

Early in Jesus's ministry, the disciples asked the Lord why he taught in parables. Jesus told them those who sought the truth would glean the knowledge he was imparting through parables, but those who were disingenuous would not understand the lesson. As he said, "This is why I speak to them in parables, because seeing they do not see, and hearing they do not hear, nor do they understand" (Matt. 13:13). In other words, they saw and heard Jesus with their own senses, but they could not perceive the truth about whom he was. Then he said something critical: "Many prophets and righteous people longed to see what you see, and did not see it, and to hear what you hear, and did not hear it" (Matt. 13:17).

Now on the road to Jerusalem, when questioned by some Pharisees when the kingdom would arrive, Jesus answered in a similar manner. He told them the kingdom was already in their midst. Then Jesus turned to his disciples and told them that soon days were coming when they would long to see the Messiah. Whether or not these two statements occurred one right after another, Luke intentionally linked them together. What's going on? If the kingdom was already in their presence, why would they long for the Son of Man?

With lesson one in place, in which Jesus established the importance of proper motivations for faithful kingdom-living, Jesus could impart lesson two. This lesson came in two parts. First is a reminder of the great privilege the disciples had in knowing Christ. Generation after generation longed for the Messiah to come and rescue them from their plight, but each passed without seeing the son of David promised by prophecy. Second, Jesus had to shatter some of their expectations about the Messiah. Though the kingdom indeed was in their midst, Christ would die and return at some point in the future. And when he returned, it would be as obvious as lightning. Yes, he would restore justice and make everything right, but not right away.

But before we dive in too deep, let's take a step back and establish some context first.

A Light for Revelation

In Western culture, we take many things for granted. It's human nature. When something has always been a part of your reality, it's easy to expect that reality will persist. We presume upon the right to freedom, clean water, and electricity. The ability to illuminate a room by toggling a switch is a luxury we all take for granted. The technology has always been a reality in our lives, so it's hard to appreciate what it would be like to live without electricity and light bulbs. But artificial light and running water amount to little compared with another privilege you might not think twice about. In fact, whether you know it or not, you are one of the most privileged persons ever to have lived. I'm not talking about money, medicine, or machinery. Even more than wealth or convenience, you probably take this privilege for granted much like I do. I'm talking about the year in which you were born. No, the specific year isn't important other than the time period it represents: you were born after the coming of the Messiah, Jesus Christ of Nazareth, who was born of a virgin, died a sacrificial death, and rose from the grave—just as the prophets said he would. Do you have any idea how privileged that makes you and me? Before you answer, recall the story of Simeon:

> Now there was a man in Jerusalem, whose name was Simeon, and this man was righteous and devout, waiting for the consolation of Israel, and the Holy Spirit was upon him.
> —Luke 2:25

Simeon had been waiting for the Messiah. He longed to see the son of David, but he wasn't alone. All of Israel lived in expectation of the Messiah. From our AD perspective, it's hard to fathom this detail. But prior to Jesus's birth, mankind had been collectively holding its breath for thousands of years in anxious desperation for salvation. Ever since Adam's taste buds triggered a flood of endorphins at the bite of that forbidden fruit—opening his eyes to good and evil but closing the door to that idyllic garden—mankind has had a dire need for a savior. Humanity longed for a Messiah who could take away its guilt and restore the once intimate relationship with its Creator.

And all of this came to a head with Simeon. The world had just endured four hundred years of silence when God ceased speaking through prophets. The Jews had rebuilt the temple after the

Babylonian siege, but now the Romans ruled the land and the people. Yet, at long last, the Savior was coming. God told Simeon he would not die before seeing what he and the rest of the world so desperately needed: the Lord's Messiah. Grasping this context is critical to understanding Simeon's reaction when he spotted Jesus in the temple. Moved by the Spirit, he snatched the Son of God from his parents' arms, praising the Lord all the while:

> Lord, now you are letting your servant depart in peace, according to your word; for my eyes have seen your salvation that you have prepared in the presence of all peoples, a light for revelation to the Gentiles, and for glory to your people Israel.
> —Luke 2:29–32

Simeon could finally die in peace because he saw the Messiah with his own eyes. He wanted nothing more than the consolation of Israel. He knew the world was a dark place, but he also knew that God had promised redemption for mankind. Now that he held the child in his arms—the fulfillment of that promise—he knew everything would one day be made right.

In our twenty-first-century mind-set, we rarely think twice about the privilege of Jesus. We take for granted that he came, died, and rose from the dead. In the Western consciousness, it's a given, just like electricity. Yes, the world is still messed up, but now there's a way to reconciliation. There's a way to heaven. And his name is Jesus. But imagine living like Simeon lived—in constant suspense, hope, anguish, and anticipation. When one loses electricity, he receives a reminder of what it would be like to live without light at the flip of a switch. Put yourself in Simeon's shoes, and it will have the same effect. Don't take for granted the privilege you have to know Jesus and to walk in his grace. Generations before you longed to see the Messiah. As Jesus himself said, "Blessed are the eyes that see what you see! For I tell you that many prophets and kings desired to see what you see, and did not see it, and to hear what you hear, and did not hear it" (Luke 10:23b–24).

We don't have Jesus with us in the flesh, but we have his revelation, his historical account, and, most importantly, his grace. Sadly, the Pharisees did walk in Jesus's presence, but they couldn't recognize what was right before them. Here's what Jesus said to them:

> Being asked by the Pharisees when the kingdom of God would come, he answered them, "The kingdom of God is not coming in ways that can be observed, nor will they say, 'Look, here it is!' or 'There!' for behold, the kingdom of God is in the midst of you."
> —Luke 17:20–21

The religious leaders wanted Jesus to tell them when the kingdom of God would show up. They believed that the Messiah would appear once and then immediately overthrow all secular nations and establish a divine kingdom on earth. In their minds, the Messiah was to be a military and political leader.

They were not completely wrong. Jesus will one day overthrow all the nations of the world, but the point Jesus asserted is that God's kingdom has *already* arrived. Read what he said to his questioners: "Behold, the kingdom of God is in the midst of you" (Luke 17:21). Do you see the irony? The Pharisees were inquiring of the King when the kingdom would come. They directed their question about the arrival of the kingdom to he who had already arrived. The Pharisees were looking right at Jesus, but they couldn't perceive what they saw (which was exactly what they were looking for). That's why Jesus said, "The kingdom of God is not coming in ways that can be observed" (Luke 17:20).

By the world's rationale, you don't measure kingdoms by one man; you measure them by the number of chariots, soldiers, arrows, and swords. The bigger, the better. But in God's kingdom, we should be concerned with only one person: Jesus Christ. When Mary conceived Jesus as a virgin, God's kingdom on earth began.

Christ Will Return

No doubt this truth about Jesus excited the disciples. Their leader was the Messiah! Finally, Israel would have rest from her enemies. At last, the Romans would no longer oppress God's people.

Not so fast.

Jesus knew the messianic expectations of the Jewish people, so he attempted to curb their excitement. Most of what follows in this lesson flew over the heads of the Twelve. If it did not, they would not have been depressed, surprised, and defeated by the crucifixion. They would have expected it. As Jesus said, "But first [The Son of Man[16]] must suffer many things and be rejected by this generation" (Luke 17:25). Now, this is not an explicit prediction of execution since one can suffer and not die, but as we will see in lesson ten, Jesus will explain later on that he would die. And yet, here the Lord implied execution too when he discussed his absence. He said, "The days are coming when you will desire to see one of the days of the Son of Man, and you will not see it" (Luke 17:22). Why would he say such a thing? Only two explanations work. One, he was not the Messiah. Two, he would leave the disciples. But since he had just told the

---

[16] Jesus referred to himself as "the Son of Man" over eighty times in the four Gospels, more than any other title. In using the phrase, Christ alluded to the apocalyptic divine human prophesied in Daniel 7.

Pharisees the kingdom was in their midst, the latter is the logical assumption.

Jesus told them this for at least two reasons. One, again, is so they wouldn't take for granted the time they had with the Christ. Second, he told them this so that in the face of persecution and injustice they would not lose heart, knowing that he would return to defeat evil once and for all. The disciples needed to hear this message because of the whirlwind they were about to experience. In just a couple of weeks, they would find themselves in Jerusalem as disciples of a crucified rabbi accused of treason against Rome. With their leader dead, they would fear for their own lives as followers of a convicted man. But even after the resurrection and Jesus's appearances to the disciples, life wasn't all peaches and cream. In fact, if anything, it only got harder. They would face persecution, arrest, flogging, and censorship. But the disposition of the disciples changed dramatically because of the hope they had in Jesus's return. In fact, Jesus told the disciples it was better for him to go away. It seems strange, but here's what he said: "It is to your advantage that I go away, for if I do not go away, the Helper will not come to you. But if I go, I will send him to you" (John 16:7). With Jesus in heaven, the Spirit came to dwell in the hearts of the believers, empowering them to accomplish great things for the kingdom. This is exactly what Jesus was trying to tell the Pharisees. His kingdom was not an earthly one, as we finite beings think of a kingdom. Instead, the kingdom is spiritual.

Yet even with the Spirit indwelling believers, the ubiquity of sin, illness, and injustice can become overwhelming. It might be tempting to resign oneself to fate and give up fighting against evil. Anticipating these tendencies, Jesus told the disciples that he would return. If Jesus's incarnation as a child in Bethlehem was his first revelation to the world, his second will be less clandestine. He won't come quietly as an infant born in a manger. Jesus said, "As the lightning flashes and lights up the sky from one side to the other, so will the Son of Man be in his day" (Luke 17:24).

Jesus used the Pharisees' inquiry as a teaching opportunity for the disciples, describing the nature of his second advent. In short, it will be sudden, unexpected, and violent. Like Noah and the flood, and Lot and the destruction of Sodom and Gomorrah, Christ will return to earth in a way that will catch the unbelieving population off guard (Luke 17:26–30). Further, he will return to punish an unbelieving world. While Jesus implied that the believing community will be spared from the impending judgment—a catastrophe far worse than a global flood or a little fire and brimstone—he made these statements so his followers wouldn't be confused about the Second Coming. Jesus wanted to ensure that the disciples wouldn't quit after his death. He wanted them to see that his death was just the beginning.

What We Demand When We Demand Justice

Now, you might be wondering how any of this applies to you. You already know Jesus ascended to heaven and is coming again. None of this is new. I submit to you that we need this lesson just as much as, if not more than, the disciples did. We may know by intellect that Jesus brought a spiritual kingdom to earth and that he will return one day. But how many of us still desire the same type of Messiah that first-century Israel longed for? We want power and justice and external peace, and we want it now. The problem, though, is that if the world were fair, I would be hanging on a cross instead of Jesus. Because just as much as my enemies, I have sinned and strayed from God. Sure, maybe I haven't done terrible things like others have. I've never murdered, committed adultery, or rooted for the Oakland Raiders, but I have harbored hate at times. I have lusted after women.

And, according to Jesus, that makes me a murderer and an adulterer.[17] When compared to the next guy or gal, I might think I'm doing all right. But when compared to God's holiness, I'm about as far away as possible. So while we demand justice, we unintentionally bring the hammer down on our own lives. The only real difference between me and the unbeliever is that I'm covered by the shed blood of Jesus. It's not fair that our Savior suffered unspeakable agony when he was innocent of wrongdoing. But this is grace. And it's what Jesus is all about.

This is why in lesson one Jesus said to forgive ad nauseam. This is why Jesus commanded we pray for our enemies. And this is why justice is delayed. As the scripture tells us, "The Lord is not slow to fulfill his promise as some count slowness, but is patient toward you, not wishing that any should perish, but that all should reach repentance" (II Peter 3:9). Jesus is waiting for the maximum number of people to obtain salvation. He's giving humanity every chance possible to turn to him and seek forgiveness. Believe me, there will be wrath and punishment for evil, but it's not the Lord's preference. Instead, he'd rather see us covered by his unmerited favor.

So when it seems like the ridiculous brutality of this world is too much, and when the pain and suffering are unbearable, remember that Christ is coming back to restore justice. In the meantime, we have the Spirit as our counselor to help us through the dark times. You and I are living in what we will call the In-Between—the period between the revelations of Christ. We exist at a unique time when all the chips are on the table. Jesus left it all out on the field, as it were, dying on the cross for any who would believe. And he will return, as he said he would, to reap the harvest and to separate the goats from the sheep (Matt. 25:32).

---

[17] See I John 3, Matthew 5.

This reality has embedded consequences, which may account for why so many people are wont to ignore it. For you, it means living a life of faith. No, you can't do a single thing to earn salvation. Grace is, by definition, unmerited favor, but it is conditional on your accepting it. As Paul wrote to the Ephesians, "For by grace you have been saved through faith. And this is not your own doing; it is the gift of God, not a result of works, so that no one may boast" (Eph. 2:8–9). So even though you and I don't deserve grace, we receive it on the condition of faith.

But too many Christians believe faith ends at salvation when it's just the beginning. You're called to walk in faith daily. This is why Jesus spelled out to his disciples what would happen at his return. He wanted to prepare them for his absence. Now that Jesus has ascended into heaven, you and I must live our lives by faith in preparation for his return.

But we mustn't focus so much on the Second Coming that we lose sight of the here and now. Another implication of Christ's return is that we must embody the sense of urgency Jesus laid out in spreading the message to others. With the great privilege we have in Jesus also comes the responsibility to act on that information. In his absence we are responsible for advancing the kingdom of God: caring for the sick, housing the widows and orphans, sharing his love. The church is his hands and feet during the In-Between, working hard to carry out his will. Does God need us to do these things? Absolutely not. He is, after all, God. He's omnipotent and sovereign, but here's the secret: God chooses to use us.

So how should you respond in light of your newfound historical advantage? It seems overwhelming to imagine such an opportunity and burden placed on our shoulders. As a believer living between Christ's revelations, you are the hope of the nations and the envy of generations. You are the light of the world. Don't take that privilege for granted. And don't lose heart in the face of abuse, corruption, and devastation. Remember that justice belongs to the Lord, and he will return to punish iniquity.

LESSON 3
Persist through the Darkness

We would accomplish many more things if we did not think of them as impossible.
—Vince Lombardi

The Sacred Text

And he told them a parable to the effect that they ought always to pray and not lose heart. He said, "In a certain city there was a judge who neither feared God nor respected man. And there was a widow in that city who kept coming to him and saying, 'Give me justice against my adversary.' For a while he refused, but afterward he said to himself, 'Though I neither fear God nor respect man, yet because this widow keeps bothering me, I will give her justice, so that she will not beat me down by her continual coming.'" And the Lord said, "Hear what the unrighteous judge says. And will not God give justice to his elect, who cry to him day and night? Will he delay long over them? I tell you, he will give justice to them speedily. Nevertheless, when the Son of Man comes, will he find faith on earth?"

—Luke 18:1–8

Jesus knew the disciples did not yet understand the previous lesson regarding his Second Coming. So to supplement his teaching, he told them a parable in a similar vein. Although the disciples were privileged to have seen and followed Jesus, it wouldn't always feel like a privilege. At times, they would feel like widows seeking justice from an unrighteous ruler. To begin, Jesus said, "In a certain city there was a judge who neither feared God nor respected man. And there was a widow in that city who kept coming to him and saying, 'Give me justice against my adversary'" (Luke 18:2–3).

A widow in the first century resided at the bottom of the societal totem pole, and therefore the judge had no worldly incentive to deliver her justice. She had nothing of value to offer the judge. This is why, in the Law of Moses, there are so many extra protections and regulations concerning widows, foreigners, and orphans. For example, Exodus 22:22 reads, "You shall not mistreat any widow or fatherless child." Does that mean it was acceptable for the Israelites to mistreat married women and children who do have dads? Of course not. But God enacted this and other Mosaic statutes because he knew these were the people most likely to be abused and ignored. These (along with the foreigner) were the helpless of the ancient Near East. They were the underdogs, the people everyone counted out.

In sporting events, the underdogs are those who are not expected to win. This was true of the widow too. Listening to the parable, the disciples had to have been thinking there was no possible way the widow would receive the justice she sought. But as a sports fan, few things excite me like witnessing competitors overcome long odds and achieve victory. I think this is why I naturally root for the underdog (unless, of course, the 49ers are playing). Give me the washed-up boxer with nothing left, the overmatched college basketball team, and the backup quarterback. I love it when the underdog pulls through and succeeds. But what is it about comebacks that are so special?

Wouldn't you agree there's something magical about competitors who, in the throes of defeat, scratch and claw their way to victory? But as special as these sports moments are, the underdogs who overcome doubt and long odds all share some common traits.

Let's dispense with the obvious: they work hard, they don't give up, and they persist in the face of adversity. However, I submit to you that these comebacks have roots much deeper and more meaningful than what happens on the gridiron or in the ring. Before scoring any points or exerting any effort, underdogs believe they have what it takes to win, even against a formidable opponent. If they didn't believe, they would simply give up rather than continue to fight in the face of such an overwhelming deficit.

In the same way, the widow in Jesus's parable demonstrated the belief that she would receive justice despite the odds against her. Because of her belief, she persisted in petitioning the unrighteous judge. Finally, she got what she sought after. The judge said, "Because this widow keeps bothering me, I will give her justice, so that she will not beat me down by her continual coming" (Luke 18:5).

The Bible gives us examples over and over again that show how God, too, has a heart for the underdog. Sleepers, misfits, and dark horses like David, Gideon, and Esther line the Bible's pages. These men and women overcame impossible odds to obtain victory. At the synagogue in Nazareth, Jesus told the audience he was the fulfillment of Isaiah 61. He read from the scroll that detailed the anointed one's purpose: "to proclaim good news to the poor . . . to set at liberty those who are oppressed" (Luke 4:18). Doesn't this epitomize the widow in the parable? She was both destitute and oppressed.

The widow, though, was not just an underdog. *Underdog* implies a chance at victory. It assumes one is outmatched. She wasn't just outmatched; she wasn't even allowed in the competition. Underdogs in sports can work with the time left on the clock, and underdogs in movies can use the unlikely resources around them, but this widow had nothing. And yet, despite all odds, the widow persisted in her petitions even though she knew the judge had no incentive to listen to her.

You and I are just like that widow. We offer nothing to the Judge. Of our own merit, we would be doomed when it comes to justice and redemption. We cannot rely on anything inside ourselves. All we have to rely on is God's promises. Is that a scary thing? Sometimes, but it shouldn't be. If even an unrighteous judge would answer the cries of a persistent widow, will not God, a benevolent and righteous judge, answer our prayers? In Moses's message to the Israelites, he reminded the people of an important truth. He told them that God did not choose the Israelites because they were the best, the brightest, or the strongest people. He said, "It was not because you were more in number than any other people that the LORD set his love on you and chose you, for you were the fewest of all peoples, but it is because the LORD loves you and is keeping the oath that he swore to your fathers" (Deut. 7:7–8). God chose Israel because of the promise he gave to Abraham.

What Jesus was trying to tell his disciples is that it takes faith to pray, especially in light of the knowledge that we bring nothing to the table. Just like the widow, we are poor, depraved, and helpless. We cannot recompense the judge with bribes or favors. It is of no advantage to him to listen to us. The only value we have is that which God gives us. It takes faith to trust that God would listen—not because we deserve it, but because he loves us.

When Suffering Threatens Faith

If it takes faith to pray, it's especially difficult to do so when adversity impacts our lives. When we experience personal turmoil through illness, financial problems, or relational conflicts, it can be hard to believe that God really cares. In classic English wit, apologist G. K. Chesterton wrote, "When belief in God becomes difficult, the tendency is to turn away from him; but in heaven's name to what?"[18] Where would we go for comfort or restoration but to our Maker? I heard someone say expectation is the mother of all disappointment. If this is true, then those times we are disappointed with God stem from shattered expectations. Of course no one expects lung cancer or automobile accidents. No one expects his or her spouse to have an illicit affair. Nor *should* we. Yet in this fallen world, these kinds of evils exist. God is not their cause, but he can use them for growth. He can use them for good.

You might be sensing a disconnect. At the outset, we discussed the darkness present in our world today. Then we wrote about the privilege we have as people living between advents. With so much evil at work on earth, you might not be buying the whole privilege argument. It seems hard to feel privilege in the face of so much darkness, especially when that darkness directly infiltrates our lives.

Because Jesus didn't immediately fulfill their notion of whom the Messiah should be, many Jews could not accept him as the anointed one. Jesus died and yet they were still under the Roman thumb. They were still suffering. And in just a few decades after Christ's death, the temple would be destroyed, and they would be dispersed from the city of David. We Christians read and believe the same prophecies from the Old Testament as do the Jews, but we interpret them differently. The Messiah will come and set everything right, but it won't happen immediately. He will return. From the Jewish perspective, Jesus could not have been the Messiah because he didn't set everything right on earth. He didn't oust the Romans and reclaim

---

[18] G. K. Chesterton, as quoted in *Cries of the Heart: Bringing God Near When He Feels So Far* (Nashville: Thomas Nelson, 2002), 65.

Israel for the Jewish people. Take for example Isaiah's messianic prophecy in chapter 42: "Behold my servant, whom I uphold, my chosen, in whom my soul delights; I have put my Spirit upon him; he will bring forth justice to the nations" (Isa. 42:1). Sound familiar? What was the widow seeking? Justice. But looking around today, we don't see justice. We see racial prejudice, sexism, and affluenza. It didn't make sense to say the Messiah had come, because the world was still so very broken. But Jesus used the parable as preparation against these presuppositions. As we learned in Lesson 2, justice will come, but not right away.

We often have the same response. When tragedy strikes, we doubt Jesus and his promises if the pain doesn't immediately dissipate. Certainly many of these reactions are legitimate expressions of sorrow and grief, but to dwell in that state is folly considering the promise of new life in Christ.

Jesus anticipated this misunderstanding in many ways, the widow parable being only one of those instances. Luke 18:1 is unique in that it is one of the few parables that explicitly state why they were given. The verse reads, "He told them a parable to the effect that they ought always to pray and not lose heart." Did you catch that? He did not want them to lose heart. Jesus knew his disciples were going to suffer in their ministries following his death, and it would be easy to grow weary and turn away from the truth.

This begs the question. Why? Why didn't Jesus just set everything right at his first coming? Why didn't he destroy the infidels, the pagans, the unclean people? Peter, the elder statesman of the church, an audience member for the parable, and disciple of Jesus, answered this question for us:

> The Lord is not slow to fulfill his promise as some count slowness, but is patient toward you, not wishing that any

should perish, but that all should reach repentance. But the day of the Lord will come like a thief, and then the heavens will pass away with a roar, and the heavenly bodies will be burned up and dissolved, and the earth and the works that are done on it will be exposed.
—II Peter 3:9–10

I can't help but assume Peter had Jesus's parable in mind when he wrote these words. God is waiting in patience that *all* might turn away from their sin to him. In the interim, the evil unleashed upon earth at Eden continues to fester and infect everything it can. Since the fall, sin has always plagued the earth, but we have the revelation of Christ. While on earth, he fulfilled his promises: he predicted his death and resurrection. So we have every reason to believe he will fulfill the rest of the prophecy concerning the Messiah at his Second Coming. This is faith: relying on the promises of God in the face of adversity.

So, yes, we live in a privileged time, but we also must suffer. Jesus said, "Whoever does not bear his own cross and come after me cannot be my disciple" (Luke 14:27). Not exactly the cheeriest statement, is it? Jesus didn't want to sugarcoat reality for his followers. Because the world is embroiled in sin, it rejects the things of God. The world cannot embrace its antithesis without compromising itself—without fundamental transformation. This is why Jesus told Nicodemus he must be born again. In turning to Christ, we cast off the world and embrace the godly. As a result, the world rejects us, ridicules us, dismisses us. But it's not just we who suffer. Peter wrote that God "is patient toward you" (II Pet. 3:9). The root of the word *patient* is *pati*, a Latin word meaning "to suffer." This is why the King James Bible and others translate patience as "long-suffering." As we suffer, God suffers with us, "not wishing that any should perish."

The widow, in the end, received justice because she continued in the faith that the judge would grant her request. Jesus told the Parable of the Persistent Widow to dispel the common Jewish notion that he, as the Messiah, would restore the world immediately. He taught his disciples to keep the faith, which leads to persistence in the face of suffering.

The Freedom to Believe

This sort of belief is what I would call tenacious faith. It's a belief that spurs people to dig in, hold on, and refuse to quit. I'm willing to bet that there's some sort of pressing issue in your life. Maybe something that keeps you up at night or a constant problem that will not seem to go away. Have you ever been so stressed about a difficulty that you couldn't sleep? Maybe it's relational, financial, or even a loss of some kind. The list could go on and on, but the fact is that everyone goes through pain, suffering, or injustice at some point in his or her life. Just like a physical wound, the problem screams for attention, nagging you at every turn. Yet the emotional wounds hurt the most. What can be done about the plight of mankind in human suffering? I think C. S. Lewis said it best: "We can ignore even pleasure. But pain insists upon being attended to. God whispers to us in our pleasures, speaks in our conscience, but shouts in our pains: it is his megaphone to rouse a deaf world."[19] God wants people to come to him and trust him when they experience pain and suffering. God wants you to believe. He wants nothing short of tenacious faith on your part.

When adversity crashes into our lives, the proper response is to turn to the Lord. Embracing God only in emergencies is a recipe for

---

[19] C. S. Lewis, *The Problem of Pain* (New York: Macmillan, 1986), 93.

poor spiritual health; it's like treating God as a last-ditch effort. However, countless people have found the Lord in the midst of that ditch. In embracing the power of the Almighty, people in adverse conditions often develop a widow-like, tenacious faith, believing they can achieve amelioration or peace from the issues plaguing their lives. This is the sort of lifestyle that ought to define a believer. Yes, the Christ follower should expect a life of struggle. If nothing else, the believer struggles daily against the sin nature of the flesh that's constantly working against the power of the Spirit in the believer's life. Therefore, in the midst of struggle and suffering, Christ expects us (the church) to have tenacious faith. You heard that right. Jesus expects something from you if you follow him: belief.

As Jesus demonstrated in the Parable of the Persistent Widow, to continue in prayer is to continue in faith and to trust in God's ability to intervene. To follow Christ with tenacious faith is to live a life like the widow in this story. She was in some sort of desperate situation, or as we would say in the South, "Someone did her wrong." So without hesitation, she continually went to the king day after day after day. She was persistent. She wouldn't quit. Why? At what point does a person begin to think her efforts are useless? How much courage did it take to stand before the king with such a request anyway? Even more, how much tenacity would it take to approach the king day after day with the *same* request? At some point, wouldn't you think, *I'm getting nowhere, and I'm irritating the king*? Not this woman. She believed the king could solve her problem. She believed that through her persistence, her injustice and pain could come to an end. She was right.

Jesus explained that the king didn't grant the widow's request for justice because he had compassion or cared about her case. The king moved in this poor woman's life because he was annoyed. If a carnal king will deliver justice to this tenacious widow, then how much more will a loving God move on behalf of his children who persist in faith? This is the point of Jesus's parable. If you would like to know what the believer's life should look like, look no further than this widow. Like this woman, our faith should fuel our actions. It should drive us to seek God and continually knock on his door. Our faith will effect change because the King has all the power and ability to move on behalf of his children. That's right, God responds to your faith.

Now I am keenly aware that making such a claim can be somewhat unpopular in the theological arena of evangelicalism in North America. On one hand, many may fear I'm about to suggest that we can somehow boss God around with our faith. On the other hand, many may claim I am on the edge of denying God's sovereignty, depicting him as a know-nothing wimpy god. I assure you neither is true. For some reason, we have a tendency to push people into theological extremes in order to make sense of certain positions. All I am teaching here is what the Lord taught in the passage above: your faith—tenacious faith—is your possession and responsibility. God does not give you faith—he doesn't force you to believe.[20] God pursues you and draws you to him, but it's up to you to respond. You have the freedom to trust in the Lord or not. Certainly this is true in regard to salvation, but it's also true in the daily walk of the believer. When injustice crashes into your life, will you persist in your faith? Or, as Jesus asked: When he returns, will he find faith on earth?

---

[20] See Romans 4:19–20, Hebrews 11:7, James 2:22. These passages teach that faith is a possession of the individual. In this way, faith is a dimension of human freedom. As faith is the condition of salvation, it also stands to reason that a person is accountable for his or her faith in the Son of God. This is not to say that God has nothing to do with a person's faith. God stirs the sinner to belief through the preaching of the Gospel and the convincing and convicting power of the Holy Spirit. A depraved sinner cannot initially come to faith unless the Spirit of God is drawing the sinner unto Jesus.

LESSON 4
Religion Is Not the Solution

Christianity is one beggar telling another beggar where he found bread.
—D. T. Niles, *New York Times*[21]

The Sacred Text

He also told this parable to some who trusted in themselves that they were righteous, and treated others with contempt: "Two men went up into the temple to pray, one a Pharisee and the other a tax collector. The Pharisee, standing by himself, prayed thus: 'God, I thank you that I am not like other men, extortioners, unjust, adulterers, or even like this tax collector. I fast twice a week; I give tithes of all that I get.' But the tax collector, standing far off, would not even lift up his eyes to heaven, but beat his breast, saying, 'God, be merciful to me, a sinner!' I tell you, this man went down to his house justified, rather than the other. For everyone who exalts himself will be humbled, but the one who humbles himself will be exalted."

—Luke 18:9–14

---

[21] David Black, "The Callings," *New York Times*, May 11, 1986; accessed November 17, 2017. http://www.nytimes.com/1986/05/11/magazine/the-callings.html.

The next lesson seems simple, but for the disciples, it may have been the most radical so far. Jesus taught that true righteousness comes from God, not from following the law. Sounds obvious, right? Maybe it does to us, but his audience needed to hear it. And though we may intellectually assent to this idea, we often operate our lives in a different manner. We don't acknowledge Old Testament law as authoritative, but some still attempt to adhere to a moral code for the purposes of obtaining righteousness on their own. To illustrate his point, Jesus told a parable about a Pharisee and a tax collector, both of whom visited the temple to pray. Jesus said, "The Pharisee, standing by himself, prayed thus: 'God, I thank you that I am not like other men . . . I fast twice a week; I give tithes of all I get'" (Luke 18:11–12).

Before we proceed, we must give some background regarding the setting of the parable. Jesus did not need to spell out the following, because his audience already knew these details. But for us, these facts lend some much-needed context to the parable.

It's no coincidence Jesus chose Herod's Temple as the setting for his parable. As he and the Twelve made their way south through Israel, they couldn't help but have Jerusalem on their minds. The city of Jerusalem was magnificent. Not only was it the political and economic capital of Israel, but it was also the center of religious life for Israel. Jerusalem also boasted the highest elevation in the region. This is why scripture refers to pilgrims traveling "up to Jerusalem" (Luke 18:31, et al).

But perhaps the most impressive feature of the capital city was the temple. The Talmud recalls a first-century saying: "He who has not seen the Temple of Herod has never seen a beautiful building."[22] Even modern scholars have called Herod's Temple the eighth wonder

---

[22] B. T. Bava Batra 4a.

of the ancient world. Truly, the temple was the pride of the Jewish people, and it's no wonder they felt God's presence when they approached the city and the temple. They believed the closer a person got to the innermost temple chamber, called the Holy of Holies, the closer one moved toward God. Indeed, scripture tells us God's presence rested inside the Holy of Holies and over the Ark of the Covenant.[23]

Notice in the parable the Pharisee was standing alone. This is most likely the case because he was in the least occupied place of the temple, the court of Israel. Only Jewish males who were ceremonially clean and brought a sacrifice could proceed to this inner courtyard. Here priests stood atop a huge ramp where the brazen altar rested, continually sacrificing animals on behalf of the Jewish people. Further inward stood the actual temple building containing the Holy Place and the Holy of Holies, but only certain priests were permitted inside of the Holy Place at various times, and only the High Priest could enter the Holy of Holies once a year. Therefore, this Pharisee was spatially as close as a non-priest could be to God's presence inside the Holy of Holies.

This is an important detail to note because standing in the court of Israel meant you had it going on. You checked all of the Mosaic boxes and had the privilege to approach very near to God's presence. It's because of this that the Pharisee had the confidence to pray his bombastic prayer, thanking God that he wasn't like all of the sinners he knew.

Sinners like the tax collector. About him, Jesus said, "Standing far off, [he] would not even lift up his eyes to heaven, but beat his breast, saying, 'God, be merciful to me, a sinner!'" (Luke 18:13). If the Pharisee was as close to God as possible, the tax collector stood far away. So where was he anyway?

---

[23] E.g., I Kings 8:10–11.

In Jesus's day, as pilgrims entered the temple, they would find themselves in a courtyard called the court of the Gentiles. This massive area was a general plaza for the Jews. Here they would congregate for various reasons—to hold meetings, to fellowship, and often to do business. This is where Jesus famously drove out the moneychangers two different times in his life. The court of Gentiles was busy with activity as Jews from all over prepared to enter the temple. However, this was as close as the non-Jews could go—hence the name.

The path for Jews who wanted to move beyond the Gentile court and enter Herod's Temple depended upon gender. The women could only travel as far as the court of women. They would climb steps on the northern side of the temple leading up to a terrace where they would serve as a choir, singing along with the Levites in the courtyard below.

Men would enter the court of women via the Beautiful Gate on the east side. This was the location of the famous beggar in Acts 3 whom Peter healed. As men entered the lower level of the court, they would be greeted with sounds of worship and the smell of sacrifice. At this point, a worshiper would experience a sense of wonder as he approached the inner court.

Since the tax collector was "standing far off," he was likely standing at the easternmost side of the court of women, as far as possible from the Pharisee and yet still within the inner courts. Or perhaps he was standing in the outer court, the court of the Gentiles, looking through the Beautiful Gate.

The full force of the parable cannot be grasped without such an intimate knowledge of temple life—the setting for the story—all of which would have been common knowledge to the first-century Jew, and especially to his initial audience as related in verse 9: "He also told this parable to some who *trusted in themselves* that they were *righteous*, and *treated others with contempt*" (Luke 18:9, emphasis added). Jesus played on these biases to challenge the popular beliefs about intimacy with God. Don't get me wrong, the primary beneficiaries of the parable were the twelve disciples, but Jesus directed the lesson at the religious elite.

The Pharisees were these religious elite. They had the answers. They knew Yahweh and were able to teach others how to follow the law. Tax collectors, however, were considered traitors and sinners of the highest order. They worked for the Roman occupiers to extort as much money as possible from their own people. Fellow Jews considered them dishonest and depraved.

With this context in mind, we can see the irony in the Lord's parable. In the eyes of men, the closer a person could travel into the temple, the better off he must be spiritually. The Pharisee had the right pedigree and credentials, yet he had no faith and would be condemned before God. On the other hand, the tax collector had no part in God's kingdom according to Jewish opinion. If he had even tried to go into the inner court, he might have been arrested. Yet he had faith and was justified before a holy God. The Pharisee was prideful. The tax collector was humble. The Pharisee had faith in himself while the tax collector acknowledged his need for mercy.

Jesus demonstrated the relationship between faith and a spiritual connection with God, something the Pharisees were wont to discount. He depicted two men with very different attitudes in regard to how they related to God, and he knew that intimacy, not proximity, with the Father would be an essential element of the disciples' faith. The only way to possess such a relationship is with a posture of humility. God won't use the proud, but he readily accepts the humble. This is the key to drawing near to God. The Pharisees sought proximity to God in the temple when, instead, they should have sought out intimacy.

If you look in the dictionary for a definition of *humility*, you'll see the following: "The quality or state of not thinking you are better than other people."[24] This is a good definition, but I think it leaves out a critical element. The definition describes our relation to other people—that the humble do not esteem themselves above others. But another crucial aspect is our relation to God. Compared to him, we are wretched, unholy creatures.

God Is Gracious

Perhaps no one knew this better than John Newton. You might not know the name John Newton, but I'll bet you know what he's famous for. No, he's not the love child of John Travolta and Olivia Newton-John. No, he's not the guy who makes those tasty-in-a-weird-way fig cookies. In reality, John Newton was an eighteenth-century English sailor known among his peers for his filthy mouth and love of insubordination. He was a navy deserter who contemplated murdering his own captain, and later on, he would become a slave trader. But he didn't start out that way.

John's mother, Elizabeth, had intended for John to join the clergy, but her premature death by tuberculosis when the boy was only seven years old derailed those plans. John's father, John Sr., was a sea captain and brought his son on his first voyage at age eleven. As a young adult, Newton attempted to hold to his faith, becoming, in his own words, "an ascetic."[25] He fasted, isolated himself from society, and devoted himself to the Scriptures for nearly two years. After a few more voyages, John was conscripted into the British Navy

---

[24] "Humility," *Merriam-Webster.com*, http://www.merriam-webster.com/dictionary/humility.
[25] John Newton, *The Works of the Rev. John Newton* (New York: Robert Carter, 1847), 82.

at age eighteen. Profane and aimless men filled the ships, but Newton tried his best to remain godly. And yet, in his own words, "I loved sin, and was unwilling to forsake it . . . I renounced the hopes and comforts of the gospel at the very time when every other comfort was about to fail me."[26] Thus began his descent into a hellish lifestyle.

John drifted from his mother's faith and descended into an incredible life of debauchery. He set the standard for cursing like a sailor, and he defied all authority. After deserting his post while at port in Plymouth, England, John was captured, and upon being returned to the ship, was stripped and publicly whipped for his crime. Newton then spent the entire trip to the Portuguese island of Madeira as a prisoner. Upon reaching West Africa, he was discharged in the service of a slave trader who made John a de facto slave. John spent the next several months on the brink of death by illness and malnutrition, during which time his masters mocked his misery. He described one particular incident in which his master's wife offered him leftovers from her own plate:

> Being exceedingly weak and feeble, I dropped the plate. Those who live in plenty can hardly conceive how this loss touched me; but she had the cruelty to laugh at my disappointment; and though the table was covered with dishes, (for she lived much in the European manner,) she refused to give me any more.[27]

With the assistance of his father, John eventually made his way back to England and would soon enough work his way up to be captain of his own ship. Nevertheless, he did not return to his

---

[26] Ibid., 82, 86.
[27] Ibid., 90–91.

childhood faith. He had endured several metaphorical storms, but it was a literal storm that would cause him to cry out for mercy. Prior to becoming captain, he and his ship encountered a squall on his voyage back to England. The crew struggled against the wind and waves for days, including a stretch in which John tied himself to the pump to prevent washing overboard. After a brief rest, he took the helm and did his best to navigate for eleven consecutive hours. It was in the middle of this crisis that John remembered the faith he had abandoned. John recalls having shouted, "Lord, have mercy upon us."[28] A starving crew and wrecked ship arrived in Ireland two weeks later.

Although his reacquaintance with Christ was not immediate, the storm began to stir something inside of him. Within a few years, health issues grounded Newton, and he began to study more carefully the Word of God. In 1773, over two decades since he had endured that terrible storm, Newton penned these lyrics to accompany his sermon:

> Amazing grace! (how sweet the sound)
>   That sav'd a wretch like me!
> I once was lost, but now am found,
>   Was blind, but now I see.
> Thro' many dangers, toils, and snares,
>   I have already come;
> 'Tis grace hath brought me safe thus far,
>   And grace will lead me home.

In writing the words to perhaps the most famous song on the planet, Newton recalled his days at sea in which God physically

---

[28] Ibid., 96.

spared him from the storm, but also led him down the path of spiritual conversion. Newton, before he would finally turn to God, had to admit that he was a wretched mess of a man. As he wrote in a letter after the incident, "I thought, if the Christian religion was true, I could not be forgiven; and was, therefore, expecting, and almost, at times, wishing to know the worst [of the storm and his impending death]."[29] Newton thought there could be no redemption for him because of the life he had lived. Although Elizabeth had no way of knowing what would become of her son the day he was born, she and John Sr. aptly named the boy John, a name which means "God is gracious."

Humility Is an Expression of Faith

Nearly every time I sing that line, "that sav'd a wretch like me!" I feel tears well up and a heaviness on my chest. I'm no slave trader or deserter, but I know I'm so far removed from God's righteousness that I'm much nearer to Newton than to God. Some both within and without the church might be inclined to denounce the use of the word *wretch*, claiming such a descriptor is depressing or inaccurate. They would cite God's love for his creation. They would cite our innate value as mentioned by Jesus when he said God knows the number of hairs on our heads (Luke 12:7). These things are true. God's love for us is endless, and because we are his creation and made in his image, we do have intrinsic value.

And yet, the acknowledgment of our wretchedness is still an accurate reality. Isaiah tells us our righteousness amounts to filthy rags (64:6). Jesus told his disciples, "Out of the heart come evil thoughts" (Matt. 15:19). This description is a faithful depiction and

---

[29] Ibid.

an explanation of evil in the world. Cain butchered his own brother out of jealousy. King David murdered his mistress's husband. Nonetheless, the moral and societal ills we see all around us should, in a deranged sense, give us comfort. Why? Because God gives mankind agency to choose obedience and to choose love. Without that ability, could real love really exist? Were choice not possible, could a man or woman enter into a genuine love-centered relationship with God?

Knowing that evil comes from man and not from God gives us recognition that there's a source of good. Even the mere acknowledgment of evil is an allusion to good, because how can evil exist but not good? So many unbelievers (and even we within the body) question God in the face of evil. Atheists like to use evil as proof of God's nonexistence. But again, the acknowledgment of evil is simultaneously an affirmation of good. When questioning God's existence in light of the presence and prevalence of evil, the questioner betrays himself by smuggling into the query an "oughtness"—some type of standard for reality. He or she acknowledges the world is not the way it should be, meaning there exists some kind of utopian prospect for morality. The only perfect standard, then, is God.

The fact that we are indeed wretches is a good thing because it forces us to rely on something outside of ourselves—the shed blood of Christ—for salvation. It is an acknowledgment that we ought to be a certain way, and we need God and his perfection to rectify it. This acknowledgment of our wretchedness is an expression of humility.

True humility establishes our proper place in relation to God and to others, and such a posture is a requirement for being used by God. As Jesus said, "All those who exalt themselves will be humbled, and those who humble themselves will be exalted" (Luke 18:14, NIV). As we see in Jesus's parable, pride results in self-justification while humility acknowledges the need for a Savior. In some respects, it's counterintuitive to think humility is a prerequisite for making a difference in God's kingdom. We expect brazenness, confidence, and boisterousness from those who intend to change the world. We want our leaders loud and proud, never admitting defeat and never showing weakness. Jesus, though, showed us a different way, not only with words, but also in his lifestyle. Jesus was the ultimate example of humility. He was born in a cave,[30] and his crib was a feeding trough. He lived a quiet life in Nazareth before beginning his public ministry. He performed a servant's task in washing his disciples' feet. He died a criminal's death, and he was buried in a borrowed tomb. In Jesus's humility we see a blueprint for advancing the kingdom.

In addition to the way he lived his life, Jesus gave his disciples another example of humility through the parable of the Pharisee and the Tax Collector. He ended the story by saying, "I tell you, this man [the tax collector] went down to his house justified, rather than the other. For everyone who exalts himself will be humbled, but the one who humbles himself will be exalted" (Luke 18:14). Notice that word, *justified*? Although the term is theologically loaded, it simply means that one is declared righteous by God. But how could the tax collector be righteous? He didn't pay tithe or fast twice a week. But he *did* have what God requires: a humble spirit. Paul wrote in Romans, "For we hold that one is justified by faith apart from works of the law" (3:28). The Pharisee relied upon his works. The tax collector exhibited faith through humility.

It's because of our tendency to cling to empty religion and ceremony that we often think once we get our act together, we'll start serving the Lord. Once we manage to go to church more, curse less,

---

[30] As Justin Martyr opined.

be more generous, beat that addiction, or whatever else, *then* we'll be ready to turn back to Christ. What we have to remember is that we cannot clean up our own messes. We need the grace and mercy of God to intervene in our lives. It's why that Pharisee was able to get into the holiest regions of the temple and still miss the mark where his heart was concerned; and yet the tax collector was met by God right where he was. God doesn't expect or want us to come to him "perfect." Truth is, we are all broken, and owning up to our ineptness is critical. As Jesus said to the Pharisees, "Those who are well have no need of a physician, but those who are sick. Go and learn what this means: 'I desire mercy, and not sacrifice.' For I came not to call the righteous, but sinners" (Matt. 9:12–13). If you were able to clean up your act—to become righteous or holy on your own—why would you need God? Just as a healthy person rarely goes to the doctor, the self-righteous rarely turn to God.

I've heard it said that the Bible is a collection of books containing no heroes, just broken men and women, until Jesus arrived on the scene. I don't know if I agree, but if there's one man who didn't have his act together, it was Moses. On the lam from Pharaoh who sought to take his life, Moses fled to Midian. He had attempted to speed up God's deliverance by killing an Egyptian, possibly thinking the death would spark insurrection. Instead, it meant exile for this once prominent man. In the wilderness, while Moses was licking his wounds, God showed up in a burning shrub. This is the lowest low Moses had experienced. So naturally it was at this point that God called him. Moses was a murderer and a man who had lost confidence. He was once wealthy, living a palace life as the son of Pharaoh's daughter. Now he was a humble shepherd in the middle of nowhere.

So when God called Moses to lead the people out of Egypt, Moses politely declined. "Who am I?" Moses asked God. God essentially told him it doesn't matter who Moses is. What matters is who God is. He can do great wonders and use whomever he chooses, weak or strong. He could've used Moses when he was brash and overconfident, but he chose to wait until Moses was at his most vulnerable.

There may not be any heroes in the Old Testament, but Moses sure comes close. And yet, he started out as a broken shell of a man, who by no means had his act together. This is an important lesson for us to learn. Advancing God's kingdom doesn't require brains. It doesn't require brawn or charisma or a Nazirite vow. It requires faith—faith that God can use you where you are despite your limitations. The scripture tells us God "chose the foolish things of the world to shame the wise; God chose the weak things of the world to shame the strong" (I Cor. 1:27, NIV). This pattern is repeated often throughout the Scriptures. God used Mary, a young woman, to bear the Savior. He used Gideon, one of the least likely men, to lead Israel in battle. He chose Samson, an impetuous, rebellious man, to bring shame upon the Philistines. He chose Mary Magdalene, an unreliable witness, to be the first to discover the empty tomb of Christ. More often than not, our efficacy in the kingdom is limited only by ourselves.

Humility Will Draw You Nearer to God than You Ever Imagined

I (Andrew) have a confession. It's a bit weird, I'll admit, but it's true. Are you ready?

I'm jealous of Moses.

Weird, right? No, I'm not jealous of all the crazy stuff he had to endure in Egypt and in the wilderness with Israel. I probably would've lost my cool sooner (and more often) than he did. But what

I am jealous of is Moses's intimate relationship with God. This man, who started out as a scared, self-conscious killer, developed perhaps the most intimate relationship any human has ever had with our Creator. He had countless one-on-one audible conversations with God. He spent days with God on Mount Sinai. And when he died? God himself buried him. The scripture tells us Moses went alone on the mountain to get a glimpse of the Promised Land before dying. Then verse 6 reads, "He buried him" (Deut. 34:6). If Moses was alone with God, who, but the Almighty, could have buried him?

Although I'm sure I'd be scared out of my mind, I'd love to hear God's audible voice just once. We will one day, and that thought excites me. We might never be as close to God as Moses was, but living humbly is one of the best ways to draw nearer to God than you ever imagined possible. The prophet Micah wrote, "What does the LORD require of you but to do justice, and to love kindness, and to walk humbly with your God?" (Mic. 6:8). Did you catch that? Walking humbly with God is a requirement. It's not optional, it's not secondary. I love that phrase—"walk humbly"—because it's a great metaphor for our relationship with God and with others. As we go about our day in our interactions with God and others, we should exhibit humility. As we do so, it opens our hearts to draw near to God.

If we're going to grow spiritually, then we must come to God on our knees. If we're going to truly know the Father and experience spiritual enrichment and connection, then we must approach him with humility and authenticity. This is the sort of attitude and approach toward our heavenly Father that actually moves the kingdom forward. But when I think God is somehow impressed with my own goodness, I lack the sort of connection with him that powerfully transforms people's lives. When I compare myself to people I think are less spiritual, I have disqualified myself from being used as God's tool for kingdom building. When I think my churchy background makes me morally superior to others, then I lack the heavenly focus required to live a missional life. In these moments when I think I'm good, I fail to approach the Almighty with the sort of faith he honors. Instead, we ought to be more like the humiliated tax collector. We ought to rest in God's grace, lean on his acceptance, and depend on his forgiveness. Like John Newton, we ought to be fully aware of our failures, shortcomings, and utter wretchedness. This is the sort of faith that moves mountains on behalf of the kingdom of God here and now.

I know what you may be asking: "How can a faith expressed through humility ever really do anything?" Exactly! This is the whole point of the parable. When we realize we are but dust, then we are positioned to be used for his greatness. In that moment, we arrive at the same understanding John Newton had acquired when he famously said, "Although my memory is fading, I remember two things clearly. I am a great sinner and Christ is a great Savior."

LESSON 5
Stop Working for Something You Cannot Earn

*Words of wisdom are spoken by children
at least as often as scientists.*[31]
—James R. Newman

The Sacred Text

Now they were bringing even infants to him that he might touch them. And when the disciples saw it, they rebuked them. But Jesus called them to him, saying, "Let the children come to me, and do not hinder them, for to such belongs the kingdom of God. Truly, I say to you, whoever does not receive the kingdom of God like a child shall not enter it."

—Luke 18:15–17

Amidst all the parables and stories Jesus told his disciples on the journey to Jerusalem, a real life lesson presented itself. Jesus grabbed hold of the opportunity and used it as a teaching moment for his disciples.

In just a few days, the Messiah would enter the city of David and be hailed with hosannas. Known as Palm Sunday, this day would

---

[31] Edward Kasner and James Newman, *Mathematics and the Imagination* (Mineola, New York: Dover, 2001), 23.

signal the start of Passion Week—the final week prior to the crucifixion of Christ. With time fleeting, the events in this travel narrative were the last few lessons the Lord would impart to his disciples. So they had better be good, right? Soon, the resurrected Christ would task the disciples with taking his message to the entire world, and they would need all the instruction they could get.

What quality would they need in order to make their mark on human history? Armies and political power? A top-level education? Mountains of money? If you've been following along, then you already know that none of these things are requirements for kingdom impact. The only requirement is faith. But in the following lesson, we see yet another facet of the kind of faith God desires. What does this history-altering faith look like? As we've seen, it looks like a widow relentlessly pleading her case to a king, and it looks like a repentant tax collector begging for forgiveness in the temple. Next, we'll learn about effective faith from a child's vantage point.

At this point in his travels, Jesus had likely reached the Jordan River and was traveling south toward Jericho. His popularity was never higher. Despite his fame, the Lord tried to keep a low profile in order to prevent undue tension with the religious leaders—a tension that would only tighten and ultimately snap once Jesus entered Jerusalem for the last time. The masses did everything they could just to get a glimpse of Israel's most famous teacher and miracle worker. Mothers and fathers left nearby villages so their kids could see and experience Jesus, and they sought blessings for their children. As Luke described it, "Now they were bringing even infants to him that he might touch them. And when the disciples saw it, they rebuked them" (Luke 18:15).

At first blush, the use of *infants* in this passage seems to indicate the children were babies. But the English Standard Version translates Luke's words as "even infants," implying children of various ages came to Jesus. Matthew and Mark also record the event, using the phrase "little children." So it's apparent that children of various ages came to Jesus. Jesus of course overruled the disciples and invited the children to him. Then he said, "Whoever does not receive the kingdom of God like a child shall not enter it" (Luke 18:17). What exactly did Jesus mean? What does it look like to receive the kingdom like a child?

Christ's Guide to Growing the Kingdom

Before answering these questions, we must first look at the story from the disciples' perspective. In case the parables of the widow and the tax collector didn't sink in, Jesus seized this moment to reinforce and flesh out another characteristic of the type of faith necessary for kingdom living. Children, widows, and tax collectors all had one thing in common: first-century Jews held them in low esteem.

As difficult as it may be for us to understand in our modern context, children didn't play the same role in first-century society as they do today. That's not to say Jews of that day didn't love or ascribe intrinsic value to their children. They certainly cared for their children; but Jewish culture demanded that its children remain seen, not heard. Put bluntly: they were to stay out of the way of adults. For this reason, the disciples saw it as their duty to keep these children away from the rabbi. Parents instructed and disciplined their children with the goal of raising productive members of society, and the concept of adolescence didn't exist in ancient culture. A child transitioned directly into adulthood. To facilitate this process, children undertook well-defined rites of passages to commemorate the change in status—a bar mitzvah, for example.

So although misplaced, there was some cultural logic behind the disciples' attempts to block the children. In addition, their contention was just as much with the parents as it was with their children. I can just see it, can't you? Jesus and the disciples settle along the road for a break when the crowds finally catch up to them. The Twelve form a human fence around their Lord to keep these joyful children at bay. What a scene! In response, Jesus surprised his followers. Despite weariness from travel and the constant barrage of people requesting healing or other miracles, and despite the lowly status of children, Jesus invited the young ones into his presence.

Jesus corrected the narrow understanding of the Twelve; he wanted to bless these children. He wanted to learn their names and laugh with them and enjoy their smiles. Perhaps there were a few shy children, and Jesus helped them come out of their shell. That a lofty rabbi would make time for young ones is incredible. His mission did not preclude him from blessing those who were perceived as less important. In fact, as Luke reminds us several times in his gospel account, these are the kind of people Jesus sought out.

The disciples learned that day that Jesus doesn't need bouncers. Perhaps I live a sheltered life, but I've never encountered a bouncer in real life. I've only seen them on television. On screen, they're usually large men whose job is to prevent drunks, underage persons, or anyone they deem ineligible from entering an establishment, and to remove those inside who become unruly. If a popular club becomes too full, they limit the number of people who can enter, and therefore, a line of eager customers forms outside. At least that's how it is on television. In a similar manner, the disciples attempted to bar parents from bringing their children to the Lord. *The Messiah doesn't have time for kids*, they must have thought. They assumed that because they were children, they were insignificant and unimportant to Jesus compared to the grand scheme of his ministry.

The great thing about God's nightclub—the kingdom—is that there is no ID check at the door. There's no Breathalyzer or occupancy limit. In reality, Jesus welcomes all who turn to him for salvation—drunks, murderers, children, saints, and sinners like me. Neither the Lord's heart nor his schedule is ever too full to receive more souls. If anything, the downtrodden and lowly are more qualified to enter the club. The Lord never intends for anyone to be turned away or blocked from his presence. Here he overcame the resistance of the disciples with a divine command: "Do not hinder them" (Luke 18:16). The Lord abhors barriers to his presence.

Sometimes, pain and suffering form roadblocks. Other times, we believe our sin is too great for God to forgive. Yet sometimes, even Christ followers erect barriers around Jesus, as was the case here in this passage. It's easy to throw stones at the disciples, but how many of us Christians do the very same thing? *He's too effeminate; she has too many tattoos; they are dressed too casually to be in the Lord's house.* Maybe you've never had these types of thoughts—if so, I applaud you—but I know I've been guilty of trying to disqualify people from the kingdom. Jesus, though, wants to destroy all hindrances to his grace.

In fact, upon closer examination, Jesus used this moment with the children to paint a picture of the salvation process for his disciples. Essentially, he's preparing them for the Great Commission. The lesson is clear: don't count anyone out in the quest to make disciples. As we see, Jesus himself called the children. In the same way, Jesus is still calling and drawing people to him, especially those we might consider outcasts. Although he no longer walks the earth, he uses his church to proclaim the gospel message and employs the Holy Spirit to draw, convince, and convict sinners from every walk of life. Jesus is like a shepherd calling for his sheep, always willing to accept people. He is knocking on the door of people's hearts for a relationship. He wants you and your neighbor. He desires the heart of your coworker. He seeks people from every tribe and nation to enter into his presence. Whether from east or west, whether young or old, rich or poor, Jesus is calling.

What a beautiful picture of the salvation process. But it's only part of the equation. There is cooperation between God and mankind when it comes to salvation, and this passage offers a glimpse into that process. Jesus calls us to himself and he offers us the gift of grace. He even works in people's hearts and lives to overcome doubt and unbelief. Yet although Jesus calls us, it's up to us to respond to that call. And Jesus welcomes those willing to come into his presence. As he said, "Let the little children come to me" (Luke 18:16). Jesus didn't force his way upon any of the children or their parents. Instead, the children ducked the disciples' defenses so they could be near the rabbi. From here, Jesus "took them in his arms" according to Mark 10. Jesus invited the children to himself and they gladly went to him. This is the core of what it means to have childlike faith. They weren't skeptical or hesitant. They didn't pose questions or list conditions. They didn't bring up past hurts, hang-ups, or philosophical objections. In other words, they didn't behave like adults. They were free and willing to be close to him. Although he calls us, he will not force us to submit to him. He didn't command the children to draw near. He never demanded, "Get over here now!"

God's invitation to humanity is like a two-way street. In one lane, Jesus is the shepherd with the missing sheep, leaving the ninety-nine to seek out the lost. Such is the picture of evangelism Jesus painted for his disciples to emulate. In the other lane, he's like the father of the prodigal son, anxiously waiting to welcome those willing to go to him. But in the end, the impetus is on the individual to receive God's grace, and Jesus told us how to accept it. He said, "Whoever does not receive the kingdom of God like a child shall not enter it" (Luke 18:17). So again we ask, what did Jesus mean?

The Young Person's Guide to Receiving the Kingdom

There are two traits common among children that, we believe, highlight what Jesus meant when he said we must receive the kingdom like a child. The first quality is the propensity to receive with enthusiasm. Children have a knack for expressing joy and excitement without reservation. Perhaps this is best typified by a short video clip that, upon its upload, quickly became an internet sensation. Although the events of December 25, 1998 in Emmaus, Pennsylvania, are cemented in internet legend, they remained secret for almost eight years. The day started out like a typical Christmas in the Kuzma household. Siblings Brandon and Rachel Kuzma began opening gifts carefully selected and wrapped by their parents. In matching pajamas, the nine- and six-year-olds tore the paper from a large box while their father, Tom, grabbed his camcorder in hopes of recording some family memories. But he couldn't have anticipated what he was about to capture. "I could not believe my eyes with what was going on, and I was hoping I wouldn't run out of tape. I've never seen this reaction in anyone before," Tom said years later.[32]

As Brandon tore away enough of the gift wrap to realize what lay beneath, his unbridled nine-year-old enthusiasm burst forth, emitting a hair-raising holler: "Nintendo Sixty-Fourrrrrrrr! Nintendo Sixty-Four!" Within seconds, Rachel recognized the gift and joined the chorus of joyful shouts. The pair had received Nintendo's latest video game console for Christmas. Brandon ran around the room, then lunged back at the box, clawing at it like an overexcited puppy burying his first bone. The siblings then jumped up and punched the

---

[32] "N64 Kids on Inside Edition," YouTube video, 1:40, posted by "N64kids," December 25, 2006, https://youtu.be/5qCNWH5KPV0?t=1m40s.

air in unison, shouting, "Yes! Yes! Yes!" And, "Thank you, thank you!"[33]

For eight years, this memory remained private, an all but forgotten inside joke in the Kuzma household. But in 2006, at the convincing of Brandon's girlfriend, Aysha, Brandon uploaded the video to his website, kuzmafilms.com, to share with the world. It wasn't long before a viewer downloaded the clip and uploaded it to a new (at the time) video-sharing site called YouTube. In less than a year, the video and its multiple iterations (replete with slow motion, sound effects, and subtitles) had been viewed over four million times. What was once just a family memory became the epitome of virality. An avalanche of attention soon followed. The Kuzma siblings appeared on *Good Morning America* and *Inside Edition*. Jay Leno featured the video on *The Tonight Show*. Even BMW showed the home movie in one of its Christmas spots with the tagline, "Remember when wishes came true? They still can."[34] Years later, Taco Bell followed suit, directing the Kuzmas to unbox the Steak Doubledilla and then reenact the hysteria from Christmas 1998.

We've all seen excited children on Christmas and even been those kids ourselves. But what caused such a commotion on the internet in reaction to the Nintendo 64 unwrapping video was the over-the-top, genuine reception to the present. Brandon and Rachel, little tikes with bright eyes, set the standard for Christmas enthusiasm. Or, as Brandon put it, "I felt like in one day I used up a couple of years of excitement."[35]

---

[33] Watch the entire scene yourself at https://www.youtube.com/watch?v=pFlcqWQVVuU.
[34] "N64 Kids in BMW Holiday Commercial," YouTube video, 0:13, posted by "N64kids," November 18, 2006, https://youtu.be/isWoLyG5dpY?t=13s.
[35] Joe Burris, "Christmas Joy Unwrapped Again and Again and Again," *Los Angeles Times*, December 22, 2006,. http://articles.latimes.com/2006/dec/22/entertainment/et-homevideo22.

Of course, Christmas presents are imperfect metaphors, but I think this is, in part, what Jesus meant when he said we must receive the kingdom like a child. If the Kuzma youngsters set the internet on fire with their explosion of joy over a video game console, how much more should we express excitement at the everlasting gift of God's grace? The uncontrolled enthusiasm and joy bursting forth from the Nintendo 64 kids is how we ought to react to the gift of redemption and reconciliation with God. Kids understand this sentiment. For adults, it's uncool to be so excitable.

Remember when King David brought, at long last, the Ark of the Covenant to its rightful place in Jerusalem? He broke down like a little kid, removing his royal clothing and dancing about the streets like a madman. His wife, Michal, upon seeing him, "despised him in her heart" (II Sam. 6:16). And when she confronted him about it, he said, "I will make myself yet more contemptible than this" (II Sam. 6:22). David allowed the joy of the restoration of God's presence in the city to overwhelm him. He didn't care who saw him or how they judged him; he wouldn't contain his enthusiasm. Children are the same way. Just yesterday after hunting Easter eggs, my daughter, upon surveying her stash and gobbling a few chocolates, spontaneously stood up and began dancing. No one nearby was playing music. We couldn't hear any rhythms. But that didn't stop her from dancing something like a cross between the chicken dance and the Macarena. She was simply filled with gladness at receiving candy and having fun outside. Dancing was her way of expressing the joy in her heart.

God offers us salvation first, then an intimate relationship with him. These are the two greatest gifts one could receive. How should we respond? Ask my daughter, and she'll tell you.

Empty-handed

The second trait children possess is the ability to accept gifts without pretense.

People often use the expression "like stealing candy from a baby" to describe an easy task. But you know what's even easier than stealing candy from a baby? *Giving* candy to a baby. What child, if offered some confection, would refuse? None that I know. No self-respecting kid says no to sugar. (And don't even give me those sugar-free things. Those should be illegal.) Try, though, giving candy to an adult and you'll get a different result. One will say she's on a diet. The next, he doesn't like candy unless it's chocolate. Another, that candy companies are evil because they make kids fat. I'd like to throw stones, but I'm just like those adults (except for the last scenario—that's just weird). When's the last time you saw an adult go nuts over a Christmas gift?

But while children epitomize enthusiasm, they come empty-handed. In fact, they couldn't even get to Jesus on their own—the parents initiated the meeting, carrying some children and leading others. Isn't that a beautiful picture? Though a person's faith is his or her own possession, external circumstances can have a tremendous effect on that faith. Whether by God's direct activity, convicting hearts and convincing minds, or the influence of other people, faith is ushered along ultimately by the work of the Holy Spirit. And yet, though there were external influences on the children, they were willing to go to Jesus in order to receive his blessing. The beauty of children is that they receive with no compunction and no pretense of paying back. They have no concept of guilt or shame or indebtedness. They simply accept the gift on faith. Just like the widow, children have nothing to offer the king. They are poor and helpless. And just like the tax collector, they are low in status.

Notice the Lord's words, "The kingdom of God belongs to such as these" (Luke 18:16, NIV). Children are innocent, trusting, and dependent. Children have nothing to offer and lack the ability to control. They are not skeptics or manipulators. They do not have hidden agendas. To all of this, Jesus said, "Anyone who will not receive the Kingdom of God like a little child will not enter it." In other words, adults must have childlike faith in order to be saved. In the same way a seven-year-old depends on his or her parents for everything, so must an adult release pride and dignity and run to Jesus. This same type of childlike faith is required not just for salvation, but also to advance God's kingdom. Of course, Christians should grow and mature in their spiritual development as they learn and apply biblical principles in their lives. However, on some level, we are called to remain children. We should all retain that dependence that comes naturally to children.

God wants us to receive his grace daily without pretense. He wants us to accept it without a sense of indebtedness. Not that we aren't indebted to God—of course we are—but we shouldn't live under the illusion that we could or should try to pay him back. That requires faith. That God would grant me grace and blessings is hard for me to accept at times. I know I don't deserve it. I keep messing up. How can God possibly keep giving grace? I don't know the answer, but I take it on faith that he will.

Children by necessity must take from their parents. Imagine a newborn saying, "I know I'm hungry, but you just fed me like an hour ago, and I still feel bad about pooping all over you yesterday. Show me how to run the washer, and I'll take care of it first." Even if infants could speak, this scenario would still be ridiculous. But that's exactly what it's like when we try to compensate our Maker. We can never pay God back for his gift of salvation. Grace by definition is unmerited favor. Receiving the kingdom like a child means accepting this grace—not just on the day we receive salvation, but every day of our lives.

Now, there's something to be said about gratitude. Children aren't always the best at expressing thanks. And doing good works for the kingdom is a great thing. But if you're doing those works to try to earn favor or pay God back, then you're not living your life by faith. You're attempting to please God by works. But remember what the author of Hebrews said: "Without faith it is impossible to please him, for whoever would draw near to God must believe that he exists and that he rewards those who seek him" (Heb. 11:6). Pleasing God is a matter of faith, not hard work.

When we receive God's grace in this manner, we affect the kingdom in two important ways. In our enthusiasm, we spread joy like a contagion, infecting the world with the love of Christ. Second, accepting grace without pretense means refusing to limit God. I wish I became perfect the day I received salvation, but I didn't. And I'm still not perfect. I'm guessing you aren't either. Therefore, we rely not on our own power but on his. And that starts with a daily acceptance of grace to forgive us when we slip up. If we're relying on ourselves to change the world, hope is already lost. But when we rely on and believe in the power of the Almighty, anything is possible. In essence then, fatalism and pessimism represent a lack of faith because these attitudes discount God's power. In contrast, childlike faith allows us to believe that God can end world hunger or eliminate racism. This isn't naivety; it's faith in an all-powerful Creator. How can one ever make a difference if he or she doesn't believe change is possible? Children are better equipped to recognize the power of the Almighty.

When Jesus arrived in Jerusalem for the last time, upon clearing the temple of the money changers, Matthew records an interesting detail. After driving out the crooks, Jesus began healing blind and lame persons, and children were shouting, "Hosanna to the Son of

David!" (Matt. 21:15). The Pharisees heard as much and chastised Jesus, asking him, "Do you hear what these are saying?" The implication is clear: you are not the son of David, the Messiah, and these kids have no business calling you such. Jesus said, "Have you never read, 'Out of the mouth of infants and nursing babies you have prepared praise'?" (Matt. 21:16).

The scene is so powerful because here we see Pharisees, men who have spent the majority of their lives studying the Scriptures, praying, and debating the law, and they couldn't understand or comprehend what children were able to recognize: Jesus was the Messiah foretold by the prophets. Jesus was literally causing people to walk, who prior were unable to do so! And yet, the children were the ones to sing praise.

God can and will use the weak. Actually, he seems to prefer them. As Paul wrote, "God chose the weak things of the world to shame the strong" (I Cor. 1:27, NIV). So as you contemplate his grace today, feel free to shout with joy and dance a jig. You have our permission.

LESSON 6
Abandon Everything to Follow Jesus

*Riches do not delight us so much with their possession,
as torment us with their loss.*
—Dick Gregory

The Sacred Text

And a ruler asked him, "Good Teacher, what must I do to inherit eternal life?" And Jesus said to him, "Why do you call me good? No one is good except God alone. You know the commandments: 'Do not commit adultery, Do not murder, Do not steal, Do not bear false witness, Honor your father and mother.'" And he said, "All these I have kept from my youth." When Jesus heard this, he said to him, "One thing you still lack. Sell all that you have and distribute to the poor, and you will have treasure in heaven; and come, follow me." But when he heard these things, he became very sad, for he was extremely rich. Jesus, seeing that he had become sad, said, "How difficult it is for those who have wealth to enter the kingdom of God! For it is easier for a camel to go through the eye of a needle than for a rich person to enter the kingdom of God." Those who heard it said, "Then who can be saved?" But he said, "What is impossible with man is possible with God." And Peter said, "See, we have left our homes and followed you." And he said to them, "Truly, I say to you, there is no one who has left house or wife or brothers or parents or children, for the sake of the kingdom of God, who will not receive many times more in this time, and in the age to come eternal life."

—Luke 18:18–30

The sixth lesson of Christ came in response to a question from a rich ruler. The man asked Jesus, "What must I do to inherit eternal life?" (Luke 18:18). We're not sure if he was present for the previous lesson on how to receive God's kingdom, but the former is related to this one. We know from Lesson 5 that there's nothing we can bring to the table, nothing we can offer God, to earn eternal life. But the Lord's response to the ruler pushed things even further, because while this man was looking for something to add to his to-do list, Jesus told him he needed to remove something from his life. He said, "One thing you still lack. Sell all that you have and distribute to the poor, and you will have treasure in heaven; and come, follow me" (Luke 18:22). The lesson here is simple: remove anything in your life that stands between you and God.

Meaningless Morality

As we saw in Lesson 5, Jesus made a pit stop along the way when crowds brought their children out to be blessed by him. Word must have spread to nearby towns and cities that Jesus was passing through. This news had reached people from every demographic too. From the poor to the powerful, everybody wanted a piece of this exciting teacher and miracle worker.

The rich young ruler[36] was among those who wanted to interact with Jesus, the famous traveling rabbi. Who was this rich young ruler? Well, unfortunately, the text never tells us, but let me be the first to offer this profound biblical insight: he was rich, young, and a ruler. Deep, right? More than likely, this man was part of a ruling counsel in one of the nearby Jewish cities. Think of him as a city councilman of sorts. Every Jewish city fell under the authority of the Sanhedrin Counsel in Jerusalem and ultimately under Rome and its governor, either Pontius Pilate or one of the Herodian kings. Clearly, this man was a part of that hierarchy. Most likely, the young man hailed from Ephraim or Jericho. He stands out because he was far ahead of the curve in regard to earning potential and power. He was a rising star.

In response to the man's inquisition regarding eternal life, Jesus recited commandments five through nine of the ten. "All these I have kept from my youth," the man said (Luke 18:21). You can almost feel the pride radiating from his response. Yet Jesus, in a way only he could do, responded in an unexpected manner. The previous statement was just a setup for what followed. He told the man to sell his possessions and give them to the poor, earning treasure in heaven as a result. You know the rest of the story. The man walked away sad because he was exceedingly rich.

The rich young ruler stands in stark contrast to characters Luke has already introduced to us. What did this man have in common with the Samaritan leper, the praying widow, the children, or the humble tax collector? Not much. The ruler had more in common with the religious elite whom Jesus continually opposed. In the same

---

[36] Although not referred to as the "rich young ruler" in the English Standard Version, multiple Bible translations, including the New King James Version and the New American Standard Bible, use this title for the man.

way, this young man looks more like the proud Pharisee praying in the temple than the broken tax collector. Jesus lived and operated in a dog-eat-dog sort of world, and the ruler was the alpha in this Darwinian society. By first-century standards, this man had it all. He embodied what most people in today's culture seem to be running after: money, a sense of youth, and power. He functioned as if the earthly world was his heavenly home. Yet, according to Jesus, he lacked the most important thing.

By all accounts, the rich man was a good man. Assuming his answers were honest, he honored his mother and his father. He did not murder, commit adultery, steal, or bear false testimony. We would probably hold up such a man as a model citizen, maybe even a model Christian. But Christ, with his ability to peer into the deep recesses of the heart, knew something was awry. "You still lack one thing," Jesus said (Luke 18:22, NIV). Isn't it interesting that Jesus used this word, *lack*, when speaking to one of the wealthiest men in Israel? The Greek source is *leipó*, a word that can also imply destitution. This rich man had untold earthly possessions, and yet Jesus was essentially calling him bankrupt. In order for the rich man to obtain what he lacked, he had to liquidate his earthly riches for the kingdom.

Too many people miss the point of this passage. They read it as a universal indictment against riches. And, indeed, Jesus even said, "How hard it is for the rich to enter the kingdom of God!" (Luke 18:24, NIV). And yet, the core of the story really has little to do with money at all. Jesus's point is that the man had placed his earthly wealth and status above God. The man may have kept commandments two through ten, and the other 604 regulations in the Torah, but he neglected commandment one: "Thou shalt have no other gods before me." The man had made his wealth and the status it earned him his god. It represented his identity and his security. But following all the rest of the commandments without observing the first commandment is meaningless.

Vegan Hamburgers

When I (Andrew) was a boy living in the Kansas City suburbs, both of my parents returned to college to finish the degrees they had abandoned a decade earlier. My mom tirelessly worked her way through pharmacy school, while my dad, answering the ministerial call, attended MidAmerica Nazarene College. When he earned his final credit, we threw a party for my dad and invited family from Missouri to attend. They all packed into our kitchen-dining room while Dad worked the grill. He was the hero of the day for accomplishing something few do—graduating college after leaving earlier in life. But he was also the hero of the hour when he swung open the screen door and emerged from the backyard with a plate of mouthwatering hamburgers and hot dogs in tow.

My cousin Jake came. He was a bit older than me, and I always relished the time we spent together. Jake was bold, hip, and hilarious, everything a shy asthmatic like me was not. But he was always kind to me and my brother, and he treated us like insiders to his magical world of awesome. So whenever the families got together, I stuck around Jake as much as I could.

At the graduation party, Jake and I chatted while filling our plates. He prepared two hamburger buns, applying tomato, lettuce, ketchup, and onion. Caught up in his conversation, he forgot to obtain the most important ingredient—the hamburger patties. Completely unaware, he closed up the tower of bread and condiments, and, pausing between statements, raised the vegan sandwich to his mouth and took a bite. After which his faced soured, and he laughed, calling out to the room, "I forgot the meat!" He had taken careful consideration to prep the bun just the way he wanted, but in his distraction had forgotten the very reason for the bun in the first place.

Attempting to live a moral life apart from God is a lot like eating a meatless burger. The bun, lettuce, mustard, pickle, and onion exist for the purpose of enhancing and complementing the beef. To have the former without the latter is ridiculous. That's why we call it a hamburger and not a bun. The rich man may have lived a moral life, but morality without a foundation of valuing God above all else is meaningless.

The Wealth Distortion Field

In 2004, the public criticized National Basketball Association small forward Latrell Sprewell for making an offhand comment during contract negotiations with the Minnesota Timberwolves. This is the same guy who had effectively been kicked off of his former team, the Golden State Warriors, for grasping the neck of his coach, P. J. Carlesimo, after the coach had criticized his passing. Sprewell clutched the throat for several seconds until teammates rushed to intervene.[37] In another incident, Sprewell threatened a teammate with a two-by-four and promised to retrieve a gun.[38] Now on the Timberwolves, the small forward was nearing the end of the season without a contract in hand. The team offered him a three-year deal worth $21 million. But Latrell outright rejected the offer, calling it

---

[37] "NBA Suspends Latrell Sprewell for Attacking Coach," *History*, http://www.history.com/this-day-in-history/nba-suspends-latrell-sprewell-for-attacking-coach.

[38] Mike Puma, "Sprewell's Image Remains in a Chokehold," *ESPN Classic*, http://www.espn.com/classic/biography/s/Sprewell_Latrell.html.

"insulting."[39] When asked about it, he had this to say:

> Why would I want to help them win a title? They're not doing anything for me. I'm at risk. I have a lot of risk here. I got my family to feed. Anything could happen.[40]

Enter well-deserved national criticism of a spoiled man child. What on earth was going on inside that man's noggin? First, Latrell was heavily leveraged with a yacht, two homes, and several luxury cars. He couldn't afford to lose a huge payday and risk defaulting on his over-the-top lifestyle. Second, he had earned $14.6 million the year he made that remark, so to him, a 50 percent reduction in salary was an unacceptable notion. This is what I call the *wealth distortion field*. Ask someone how much is enough, and the typical answer is a little more than he or she already has. Thus, you get a Latrell Sprewell who can say with a straight face that he might not be able to feed his family on $7 million a year.

But it's not just professional athletes who suffer from the wealth distortion field. In fact, if you're reading this book, you are rich yourself. Unless you're living in third-world conditions, your situation is much like the rich man's. Just the fact that you know English and know how to read tells me quite a bit about you. You have received some type of education, a luxury in the third world. This means you probably live in an industrialized society with access to modern technology and transportation. And, as a result, you probably also have abundant, clean, and safe drinking water. Those few details alone put you head and shoulders above much of the world. But you might not think you're rich. You might point to your

---

[39] Rick Reilly, "Getting by on $14.6 Mil," *Sports Illustrated*, November 15, 2004, http://www.si.com/vault/2004/11/15/8191994/getting-by-on-146-mil.
[40] Ibid.

neighbor whose house is a bit bigger, or your other neighbor who has a Jaguar is his garage. These guys are rich. Or maybe you would point to professional athletes who earn multiple millions per year. Those guys are rich. Unless you're the wealthiest person on earth, you can always point to someone with more money than yourself. This is the wealth distortion field. Just like time, money is relative. One thousand dollars on Wall Street means you're a pauper. One thousand dollars in Haiti makes you wealthy.

Many read the conversation between Jesus and the rich man and erroneously assume the passage requires all "rich" people to sell all of their possessions and give the proceeds to the poor. But many of those same people won't acknowledge that they themselves are rich by global standards. The point is not how much money you have, but rather your attitude toward money—or toward anything, really. Anything can stand between you and God, if you'll let it. Work, influence, your appearance—any of these things can get in the way. Even good things like family can become gods if they become more important than God. This is why Jesus said, "If anyone comes to me and does not hate his own father and mother and wife and children and brothers and sisters, yes, and even his own life, he cannot be my disciple" (Luke 14:26). Jesus knew that the rich man loved his money, and that's why he called him out on it.

You and I must be willing to surrender that which we cherish most in favor of God. I don't believe God wants every wealthy man or woman to sell all of their possessions, but maybe some need to do so. Yet those who derive their security, self-worth, or identity in anything but God are headed for disaster. The problem with money is that having an abundance of wealth makes it easy for one to turn from God. How often do those in want kneel in prayer that God would provide their daily bread? Meanwhile, the Sprewells of the world have enough scratch to feed their kids for a lifetime. It is for this reason Jesus said, "How difficult it is for those who have wealth to enter the kingdom of God!" (Luke 18:24).

This confounded the disciples. In response, scripture tells us the disciples were amazed and asked, "Who then can be saved?" (Luke 18:26, NIV). Such a reaction might seem bizarre to us, but not from the Jewish point of view. From their perspective, the rich young ruler had his life together. He must have been right with God. After all, just look at how God had blessed him. You see, the Jewish people viewed the wealthy as having God's favor. And why not? God blessed Abraham with vast wealth. He restored Job double his possessions at the conclusion of his trials. Isaac was rich. King David too. God blessed these upright men. As the scripture says:

> Blessed is the man who walks not in the counsel of the wicked, nor stands in the way of sinners, nor sits in the seat of scoffers; but his delight is in the law of the LORD, and on his law he meditates day and night. He is like a tree planted by streams of water that yields its fruit in its season, and its leaf does not wither. In all that he does, he prospers.
> —Psalm 1:1–3

King David laid it out for us: don't listen to the wicked, delight in the law of the Lord, and you will prosper. And we see the converse illustrated in the story of Jesus healing the blind man in John 9. The disciples asked Jesus, regarding the man, "Who sinned, this man or his parents, that he was born blind?" (John 9:2). They assumed that for the man to have been born blind, someone must have done something deserving of blindness. Jesus dispelled their karmic notions, telling them neither he nor his parents had sinned.

With this context, you can understand the disciples' reaction, but the Lord's response to their amazement is helpful: "What is impossible with man is possible with God" (Luke 18:27). What a pregnant remark! What was Jesus really telling the disciples? Quite simply, humans cannot save themselves from sin any easier than they can thread a camel through the eye of a needle.[41] And isn't that what the rich man wanted to do? Notice he said, "What must I *do* to inherit eternal life?" He wanted somehow to work his way into heaven using the law. We often fall into the trap of believing that if we somehow perform enough good deeds, God will grant us eternal life. It just isn't so. In reality, only God can save a person. Rich or poor, it's impossible for us to save ourselves. The rich, though, just might be deluded enough to think they can buy their way into heaven. (Remember Simon the Samaritan who tried to buy access to distribute the Holy Spirit in Acts 8?) With money comes power, and it's easy to equate earthly security for heavenly security.

We must be willing to give up security on earth for the sake of the kingdom. Without this attitude, is it possible to live by faith? After Jesus told the man to sell his things, he said, "Then come, follow me" (Luke 18:22b, NIV). You and I must first surrender what we've placed ahead of God in order to advance his kingdom. Can we ever make a difference in the kingdom if we value money (or anything else) above God?

---

[41] A popular but false interpretation of this passage is that Jesus was talking about a smaller gate in Jerusalem that was reserved for camels. A camel would have to be unloaded of its luggage and would have to crawl through the gate. As interesting as this sort of story may seem, it is just that—a story. No such gate existed in Jesus's day. No such gate exists today. Such an interpretation actually works against the whole point of Jesus's statement. Jesus is repeating a popular rabbinical phrase. Rabbis often used this phrase and others like it hyperbolically for teaching purposes.

How to Devote Yourself to Christ

Let us not forget that Luke is using these series of events to build a case for faith. The Lord was about to depart, and the disciples' faith would be essential in advancing the kingdom. Therefore, the encounter that took place between Jesus and the ruler was actually for the benefit of those twelve rugged followers. With this in mind, Luke made sure to contrast the reaction of the young ruler and that of the disciples when Jesus commanded full devotion.

Full devotion. Think about those words for a minute. Is that not what Jesus demanded when he said, "One thing you still lack. Sell all that you have and distribute to the poor, and you will have treasure in heaven; and come, follow me"? Allow me to paraphrase: "Get rid of all your stuff, because your stuff has become your god." There was a major barrier standing between this ruler and a life he never could have dreamed: his stuff. But full devotion is difficult, isn't it?

My wife obliged me to see the doctor about two years ago. I wasn't sick. I needed a physical. Our term life insurance had expired, and we were preparing to purchase another policy. I wasn't in horrible shape, but my body had endured a five-year lazy streak. At six feet tall, I had bumped up to nearly 240 pounds.

My doctor gave me some stark news. "Mr. Sweet, I've seen your case thousands of times. You're not horribly overweight, but you're on pace for a stroke or heart attack by your late forties or early fifties." I lowered my head at the grim outlook. But what really distressed me were the words that came next. "As a pastor, you want to serve people, but soon you won't be able to help anyone if you continue living the way you're living now." Oh my! He got my attention. In my gut, I knew what I had to do. I needed to attack the problem with total abandon. Within six months, I was down to 195 pounds.

How does a person lose forty-five pounds in six months? He

overhauls everything about his life and takes severe measures to change. I had to execute great changes to my schedule, diet, and activity. First came the discipline to go to bed early so that I could get up early to exercise. No more binge-watching Netflix into the wee hours of the morning. Then came the calorie counting. I read labels and logged data like a librarian. You'd be surprised how many calories we take in without thinking about it. Several times a day, I would step onto the scales and watch an ounce or two melt away. Then there was the daily cardio after which I walked out of the gym dripping in sweat.

But let's get real for a minute. Although my weight loss is an example of full devotion in regard to physical health, it's nothing when compared to the importance of spiritual health. But as a metaphor, it's a good example of the extreme measures necessary to achieve spiritual fitness. In the same way I attacked my love handles, devoting yourself to Jesus involves total abandonment to the plain ole worn-out sort of life we grow accustomed to.

What does total abandonment to Jesus look like? It looks a lot like getting rid of all your stuff in order to follow him. Am I actually advocating selling all of your possessions? Possibly. That depends on your attitude toward material possessions. Jesus commanded the rich young ruler to take an incredible step of faith, didn't he? After all, the man had extensive wealth. He had built his whole life around his own little empire. Perhaps he inherited his wealth, or perhaps he earned it himself. Either way, he was in love with money. He spent his days toiling to preserve that which he had and to earn even more. The man's money was his life, and it consumed his very being. He leveraged his wealth to accumulate power and prestige in his community, and he made it his life's mission to climb the governmental ladder in order to carve out his legacy. Does this sound familiar? How many people toil their whole lives to become great here on earth? How many make it their life's mission to have that dream home and retirement fund, and belong to the right social circles? In other words, we are no less addicted to stuff and empire building than the rich young ruler. Jesus's command to Western culture is the same: "Abandon your possessions! Devote yourselves to me!" Do you want to know a simple word for that? Faith.

How to Do the Impossible

We have a tendency to water down faith. The word *faith* has devolved into some sort of fuzzy Christian cliché we toss around until it has lost all meaning. (We do this with *love* too; I love my wife, and I love my iPhone.) *Faith* has been so abused it invokes either a defensive posture or a cringe. At the same time, the word has become so overused it has lost its impact, becoming no more important than a decorative picture at a Christian bookstore. Let there be no doubt Jesus called the rich young ruler into a life of faith. That faith must be expressed by total abandonment of the barriers that existed between himself and the Almighty. This is the type of faith Jesus is calling us to today. It's so much more than simply acknowledging belief in him. The faith that moves the kingdom forward stems from a belief in him so strong, its bearer will do anything to rid himself of the barriers this world has to offer. Can I tell you a secret found right here in the text? *When Jesus is our treasure—when we abandon all for his sake—he uses us for the impossible.*

I believe Jesus wanted the rich man to become a disciple. Therefore, Jesus exposed the barrier that was keeping him from genuine faith—his love for money. You see, when materials possess our hearts, we can have no part with God. On the other hand, when we're willing to give up anything and everything to follow Jesus, he will leverage that sort of faith in powerful ways. Why is it hard for rich people to enter into heaven? Because letting go of the temporal for the sake of the eternal is hard. Disregarding the material for the sake of the invisible goes against everything our flesh desires. God can save the rich and the poor. He can and will save anyone who makes Jesus his or her treasure.

This is why Peter questioned Jesus. He and the other disciples did indeed make sacrifices to follow Jesus. Peter said, "We have left our homes to follow you." The Lord's response is fascinating. "Truly, I say to you, there is no one who has left house or wife or brothers or parents or children, for the sake of the kingdom of God, who will not receive many times more in this time, and in the age to come eternal life" (Luke 18:29–30). Did I read that right? If the rich young ruler had sold his possessions to follow Jesus, would the Lord have made him richer, younger, and more powerful? If I sacrifice my Kia for Jesus, will he give me a Lexus? Not exactly.

Peter never got rich. But what did Peter do? God used him to accomplish the impossible. Peter had already trusted the Lord enough to walk on water. And he would eventually preach one of the greatest sermons in history after which three thousand people responded and were baptized. That's something only God can do in a person's life. What was going on with Peter that the Lord used him to become the leader of the early church? He had unprecedented faith. Peter abandoned all for Jesus; he treasured the Lord that much. God used Peter to advance the kingdom because Peter possessed an impossible type of faith.

If this kind of faith seems overwhelming to you, you're in good company. How on earth can you and I ever live up to such a standard? First, drop the comparison game. In ways similar to how we treat wealth, the temptation is always there to compare faiths or sacrifices. Resist this temptation. Remember that your walk with Christ is a relationship, not a contest. Second, recall what the Lord said to the disciples. *What is impossible with man is possible with God.* We can't do this on our own. Instead of trying to do the impossible, rely on God first to bolster your faith. Last, we must push aside anything that stands between us and God. This requires careful introspection, prayer, and reliance on godly mentors, because often these barriers aren't abundantly obvious to us. Sometimes, as in the case of the rich young ruler, what is most precious to us is the very thing we need to remove from our lives. Once identified, we can begin the process of selling off these possessions. In turn, the Lord will reward us with a rich and vibrant faith.

LESSON 7
Faith Leads to Extraordinary Outcomes

God has put enough into this world to make faith in him a most reasonable thing. But he has left enough out to make it impossible to live by sheer reason alone. Faith and reason must always work together in that plausible blend.[42]

—Ravi Zacharias

The Sacred Text

As he drew near to Jericho, a blind man was sitting by the roadside begging. And hearing a crowd going by, he inquired what this meant. They told him, "Jesus of Nazareth is passing by." And he cried out, "Jesus, Son of David, have mercy on me!" And those who were in front rebuked him, telling him to be silent. But he cried out all the more, "Son of David, have mercy on me!" And Jesus stopped and commanded him to be brought to him. And when he came near, he asked him, "What do you want me to do for you?" He said, "Lord, let me recover my sight." And Jesus said to him, "Recover your sight; your faith has made you well." And immediately he recovered his sight and followed him,

---

[42] Ravi Zacharias, "Think Again—Deep Questions," *RZIM*, August 28, 2014, http://rzim.org/just-thinking/think-again-deep-questions/.

glorifying God. And all the people, when they saw it, gave praise to God.

—Luke 18:35–43

Now at Jericho, Jesus and his followers were fewer than twenty miles from Jerusalem. As we saw in the previous two lessons, crowds of people surrounded the rabbi wherever he went, and as they neared the Holy City, the throngs of people only grew larger. But why? What were they hoping to accomplish? The majority no doubt were in it for the spectacle. They hung around because they wanted to see the next amazing thing Jesus would do, but they weren't willing to commit to his teaching.[43] Why not? For one, he didn't look the part. Isaiah prophesied that the Messiah "had no form or majesty that we should look at him, and no beauty that we should desire him" (Isa. 53:2). When the Jewish people pictured their Messiah, they pictured someone powerful, strong, and highly capable. As a persecuted and oppressed people, they wanted a Messiah who could come down, destroy their oppressors, and restore all they had lost. They wanted to experience the supernatural—to see, hear, and feel the power of Jesus. They wanted to sate their senses.

Jesus, though, came to earth as a meek, poor carpenter, born in a manger. He taught his followers to love those who did them wrong and to pray for their persecutors. He taught people to turn the other cheek, and that in his kingdom, the last would be first. Jesus did not appear to be one who could reign down righteous retribution, and he taught that his redemption wouldn't come instantly. It makes sense that that wouldn't be the most attractive offer to many who encountered Jesus. They wanted—as many of us still do today—a

---

[43] See John 6, in particular, verse 66: "After [Jesus's teaching on the bread of life] many of his disciples turned back and no longer walked with him."

Messiah whose power and strength could be seen and felt. But remember what Jesus said to the Pharisees? The kingdom is not coming in an observable manner.[44] Since the kingdom is transcendent, it manifests in ways not always visible to the eye. This is why Jesus said of the masses, "This people's heart has grown dull, and with their ears they can barely hear, and their eyes they have closed" (Matt. 13:15).

Even Thomas, who had been with Jesus from the beginning, refused to believe that his rabbi had come back from the dead. He demanded to see the risen Lord and his wounds before believing. Jesus satisfied Thomas's request, allowing Thomas to take him in with his entire range of senses. Not only did the doubter lay eyes upon the wounds, but he also felt them. He heard Christ's voice and smelled the aroma of the Savior. Thomas, having experienced Christ in the flesh, finally believed. In response, Jesus said, "Have you believed because you have seen me? Blessed are those who have not seen and yet have believed" (John 20:29). Jesus predicted his death and resurrection multiple times to his disciples, so Thomas should have anticipated the miraculous. In addition, all of his brethren were telling him Jesus was risen. Yet, in spite of all the evidence, he would not believe unless he looked upon Christ with his own eyes.

While Jesus was still alive, the masses approached him in the same manner. The crowd accompanying Jesus on his way through Jericho had grown large. They all wanted to see what kind of amazing miracle he would perform next. So they thronged Jesus hoping to satisfy their senses. They pressed up against him so they could catch his every word, touch his cloak, and see his next demonstration of power.

They would not be disappointed. In this lesson, Jesus demonstrated through supernatural healing the extraordinary

---

[44] See Luke 17:20.

efficacy of a person's faith. As the masses proceeded through the city, a blind beggar heard the commotion and asked others what was going on. When they told him Jesus of Nazareth was about to pass by, he seized the opportunity, crying out to the Lord for mercy. In response, Jesus said, "Recover your sight; your faith has made you well" (Luke 18:42). Then the blind man followed the rabbi and gave glory to God.

Ironically, this story of faith has become a source of doubt to some. Skeptics have attempted to attack this narrative and use it as a case study for why the Gospels cannot be trusted. Like disqualifying a witness in court, they have tried to pick apart the three different accounts of this event. In addition to the version recounted here, Matthew 20 and Mark 10 also tell a version of the healing of the blind man in Jericho. So before we proceed, let's clear up a few things.

Tackling Elephants

We'll call these issues elephants in the room, and there are four such pachyderms we need to address. Elephant one is a supposed inconsistency regarding the geography of Jericho. Several times, the gospel writers describe the city of Jericho as being "down" from Jerusalem, giving the impression that Jericho is south of the Holy City. For example: "A man was going *down* from Jerusalem to Jericho, and he fell among robbers" (Luke 10:30a, my emphasis). At first glance, this seems strange since Jericho is actually about twenty miles east and slightly north of Jerusalem. Did Matthew, Mark, and Luke not understand simple directions? Hardly. Remember that Jerusalem rests high above any surrounding cities. Therefore, this elephant is easy enough to tackle when we understand the Gospel authors were referring to elevation. Jericho sits a whopping twelve hundred feet below sea level. Modern Jerichonians affectionately call their hometown the lowest city on earth. Jerusalem, however, is roughly three thousand feet above sea level. This is why theologians refer to Luke 17:11 through 19:28 as the ascension discourse.[45] Anyone going to Jerusalem had to "go up," climbing thousands of feet to get there. From Galilee, Jesus would have traveled down into the Jordan Valley and then back up from Jericho to Jerusalem.

Elephant two is a bit more complicated. Mark and Luke tell us Jesus healed one blind man in Jericho. Matthew tells us Jesus actually healed two blind men. Why the inconsistency? How many men received their sight that day?

The third elephant centers on the blind man's name. Mark identifies him as Bartimaeus, but neither Matthew nor Luke give a name to the blind man. Why would those two exclude this guy's name?

The response to both of these last two issues is basically the same. Each gospel writer had a unique purpose for writing his account, with a specific audience in mind, and the freedom to include or exclude details as they suited his needs. Think of it this way: we don't pounce on a sportswriter for failing to describe every pitch of a baseball game. Instead, we understand that some strikes and balls are not worth mentioning. Note: these two variations do not revolve around any major theological tenet, nor do they contradict one another. Yes, Mark and Luke wrote about one blind man, but they never claimed there was *only* one blind man. Jesus healed so many people, it would have been impossible to record every one. It is as John wrote in his gospel—that the world would not be able to contain the number of

---

[45] Robert H. Stein, *Luke: An Exegetical and Theological Exposition of Holy Scripture (The New American Commentary)* (Nashville: B&H, 1992), 296–297.

books required to record every miracle Jesus performed.[46]

Mark and Luke saw something unique in Bartimaeus—something from which their audiences could benefit. Jesus did in fact heal two blind men, but the testimonies of Mark and Luke are not invalidated because they only mention one man. It just means they didn't feel that it was important to include the second man in order to get their message across. Poor guy! Then what's with Mark naming the blind man? Mark more than likely knew him or knew of him, so he included it in his account. Luke and Matthew either didn't know Bartimaeus or didn't care to mention his name. We sometimes forget the disciples were *real* people who lived in *real* time and space, in an area that wasn't very large. (The entirety of Israel is roughly the same size as Vermont.) That Mark knows this blind man's name actually adds to the validity of the account. If I said, "I have a daughter named Karis," and then turned around and said, "I have three daughters," that doesn't mean I'm contradicting myself. This is essentially what Matthew, Mark, and Luke are doing. Their accounts are from different perspectives, but they do not contradict one another.

The final elephant is what most skeptics drool over. Mark and Luke tell us that Jesus performed the miracle as he approached Jericho. Matthew wrote that the miracle happened as Jesus was leaving Jericho.[47] Surely this is a contradiction, right? Actually, all three accounts are trustworthy. The skeptic is left embarrassed when he or she learns that in Jesus's day, there were two Jerichos that made up Jericho proper. As one traveled from east to west, he would first encounter old Jericho, which boasted Old Testament ruins and was a relatively small village. (Yes, the ruins of Jericho from Joshua's day are still there!) Roughly two miles away was the new Herodian

---

[46] See John 21:25.
[47] See Matthew 20:29.

Jericho strategically built and settled by Herod the Great. In Jesus's day, this entire area was simply called Jericho. With this perspective, we can clearly see that Jesus performed this miracle as he left the old Jericho and made his way toward the new Jericho. In this way, all of the Gospel authors were right in their descriptions.

Desperate Times, Desperate Measures

With these elephants out of the way, let's turn our attention to the blind man of Jericho. Interestingly, the name *Bartimaeus* is an Aramaic rendering for the Hebrew name Ben Timaeus, meaning *son of Timaeus*. Timaeus is a Hebrew word for *unclean*. It's important to keep in mind that Hebrew names carried significant meaning as they gave insights into a person's character, purpose, or physical condition. For example, Esau was born covered with red hair so his parents named him Esau, meaning *red*. Because of this, it's likely Bartimaeus's father had some sort of physical disability or disease that prevented him from taking part in temple worship—therefore rendering him unclean according to Mosaic law. As a result, Timaeus would have been a social outcast who struggled to earn a living for his family.

But by the time Jesus strolled through Jericho, we have to presume all of Bartimaeus's family was gone considering the blind man was begging on the roadside. First-century society was inhospitable to people like Bartimaeus. There was no social safety net for the handicapped. These people couldn't work, were excluded from religious rites, and were looked upon as a social burden. Without family assistance, the disabled had to appeal to the community and travelers for daily sustenance. My guess is Bartimaeus had a life so difficult our Western minds can hardly fathom the level of poverty, ridicule, and inhumanity he experienced on a daily basis. The simple Sunday school explanations about how a blind man operated in the first century do not do justice to people like Bartimaeus who grew intimate with poverty and injustice.

But all of this suffering was about to end. The day Jesus passed through Jericho, Bartimaeus was doing what he did every day—begging. Can you imagine it? Each day after miserable day, Bartimaeus and his blind friend managed to set up shop along the travel route, hoping locals would spare a few coins to help them get by. More so, they hoped Jews en route to Jerusalem to worship would have a soft spot in their heart for this begging duo. Mark 10:46 tells us a large crowd traveled with Jesus, so you can imagine Bartimaeus's excitement when he heard the rumble of feet and voices approaching off in the distance. Perhaps he was just hoping for an abnormal haul, but Bartimaeus started asking about the crowd. It wasn't every day a huge parade marched through Jericho. *Something special must be happening.* For a moment, the blind man stopped begging for money and instead began soliciting information. *What was going on?* At last, someone in the crowd answered him: Jesus was coming through town! At this point, the Lord was nothing less than a celebrity. His fame stretched across all of Judea, Galilee, Perea (the area east of the Jordan River), and the Decapolis (northeast of Perea). Even people north of Galilee in Phoenicia recognized that the Lord was something special.[48]

For the first time in his life, Bartimaeus saw a glimmer of hope.

In response, Bartimaeus discarded any remaining shred of civility, embarrassing himself and those around him by screaming at Jesus to get his attention. "Son of David, have mercy on me!" he wailed. He may have been blind, but his vocal cords never worked better. Despite the rebuke of the crowd, Bartimaeus yelled all the more.

---

[48] See Mark 3:7–12.

What did he have to lose? He was desperate, and Jesus was his chance for healing. We might call this approach blind faith—not in the typical connotation of one lacking evidence, but of one desperate for restoration with a newfound hope in spite of barriers to belief. You see, when a person is at his most desperate moment is when he's ready to believe.

An Opportunity for Faith

In this regard, Bartimaeus's physical liability was a spiritual asset. His condition forced him to rely on the information other people gave him. Today, many with visual impairments have access to technologies like brail and screen readers that help disseminate information. Not so with Bartimaeus. He had to depend on others to tell him about Jesus's exploits. Can you imagine being Bartimaeus when the news reached his ears that a rabbi named Jesus healed a man born blind in Jerusalem? This event, recorded in John 9, took place just six months earlier and only about twenty miles from the dusty Jericho roadway on which Bartimaeus perched in anticipation. He couldn't confirm whether this Jesus guy had actually healed other blind men, but the stories had to have filled him with excitement. Nevertheless, this impairment put the blind man in the best possible condition to glorify God and to see transformation. Those with sight could more easily investigate the claims about Jesus's supernatural deeds. And if they hung around the rabbi long enough, they were bound to catch the next miracle with their own eyes. We cannot say the same for Bartimaeus, and such a limitation created an opportunity for faith.

The irony in this story lies at the heart of the man's disability. While the crowds looked upon Jesus with their physical eyes, the blind man perceived the underlying truth about the rabbi—

something the masses could not see. Identifying Jesus as the son of David was no small deal, hence the rebuke from the crowd. Everyone knew the Messiah would descend from David of the tribe of Judah. Therefore, the beggar, in using this title, was identifying Jesus as the Christ, the Jewish Messiah. This, in itself, is a statement of faith. Earlier in his ministry, Jesus cited healing as evidence that he was the Messiah when he said that "the blind receive their sight" (Matt. 11:5). He was quoting one of Isaiah's messianic prophecies. So for the blind man to use this moniker, "Son of David," was almost a dare to the Lord. *If you are the Messiah, you can heal me like you've healed others.* You see the information Bartimaeus had heard about Jesus, although exciting, had to have seemed far-fetched. Healing the sick? Restoring the lame and leprous? Who could do such things? Only one sent from God. This is why Bartimaeus called Jesus David's son; he knew only the Messiah could restore his sight. Even though he was blind, he had twenty-twenty spiritual vision because he had a good view of Jesus's identity and purpose.

When Jesus said, "Your faith has made you well," he also declared the blind man saved. Yes, he restored Bartimaeus's sight, but more importantly, he also healed his soul. As a result of this blind faith of desperation and hope, the physical and the spiritual were radically transformed.

Your Faith Impacts Others

The healing of a blind man is an incredible story, but I think one of the most powerful takeaways you and I might find in this text is the impact the blind man's faith had on the crowds. True, his faith made him well (Luke 18:42), but how did the crowd react? At witnessing the miracle, the people, who had just rebuked the man, now worshiped God as a result of his bold faith. This is our best tool for glorifying God. In displaying faith, others will recognize God's power and glory and will be compelled to worship him. Not that anything we do or say is noteworthy—we are mere pointers to God's glory. And these displays of faith need not always be grandiose moments as in the life of the blind beggar. Often, these are subtle displays of hope or courage or positivity in the face of adversity. God can use us in these moments to reveal the Spirit to those around us.

In the same instant Jesus healed Bartimaeus, those in the crowd had their eyes opened to the glory of God. Now they understood that Jesus was Lord. They believed because they saw, because they were witnesses to the miraculous. But blessed are those who believe, like this blind man, without seeing. Only a wicked generation demands a sign, especially in light of all of the evidence presented us: his majesty in creation, the beauty of love, the revelation of his word, and the historicity of the resurrection. All of these things should suffice to bolster belief. Yet, being the sensual, shortsighted bags of flesh we are, we over-rely on our eyes, ears, noses, and mouths.

As high schoolers, my best friend, Willy, and I took a Saturday to go to Grand Lake in northeast Oklahoma for a day of fun and adventure. Seriously, we were cool like that. To our surprise, we stumbled upon two twenty-foot cliffs with a pool of water resting between them. The cliffs were only about ten feet apart, and a person could easily bypass them on either side as the ground came back together. The pool of water eventually fed out to the lake. Right away, we recognized this was a prime place for either a potential injury or a boatload of fun. Later, I found out that my friend Willy was familiar with this spot, but he didn't let me know that at the time. Instead, he just looked at me and said two simple words: "You ready?" Without thinking it through, without deliberating on the potential for injury, without resting in my fear of heights, we both jumped in.

This is what blind faith ought to look like. Faith is not about recklessness, but about placing trust in Jesus who knows all things. He knows what's best for us, and sometimes, he asks us to jump when our eyes might be telling us to stay on the rocks. Are you desperate for Christ? Does your hope lie in him? Trust in Jesus to restore and rescue, and he will refresh you—like an ice-cold spring refreshes one on a hot summer day. God is calling you to something. I don't know what specifically, but I can assure you it leads to other people giving God glory. Whether he's calling you to serve in the nursery at your church or preach the Gospel to people in Mozambique, his purpose is for his people to bring him glory. Serving orphans and widows gives him glory. When you make his name known, it gives him glory. When you're transformed from the old to new, it brings him glory as well. All of this is only possible when we respond to him in faith.

As hard as it may be to think about, Bartimaeus could've stayed seated and silent on that day. He could've expressed skepticism at the information he received about the Lord. He could've said to himself, "I know people say Jesus is great, but I'm going to wait until he cures me of my blindness and then I'll believe he's the Messiah. Until then, I'm just going to sit here and keep begging." This is the attitude of too many. As Jesus is walking by, people say, "If he really cared, he would come over here. Why should I have to cry out to him and risk sounding like an idiot?"

This is why your faith matters. Christ is ready and willing to intervene in your life. He's calling and pursuing. He has laid out an abundance of evidence for people to consider and investigate. However, for those who have yet to follow him and even for Christians, he beckons us to trust him. If you're in Christ, amen! You've trusted Christ to save you, but have you trusted him enough to go where he's calling you to go and do what he's calling you to do? Christians: Christ wants to leverage our lives to impact the world, reach the lost, change the culture, help the hopeless, and bring glory to the Father. Too many of us are standing on the edge of the cliff thinking and fretting instead of trusting, worried about what others think or how our lives will change if we jump. Little do we know that, yes, the jump is scary, but there is one who is jumping in with us.

Christ is calling us to jump, but like my friend Willy, he has taken the plunge already. He's beside us the whole time. He knows that the water is deep, clean, and clear of rocks. And the water feels great. The water will bring refreshment to the weariness of life. We must trust him enough—without all of the facts, figures, and information—to jump in.

That we, when everyone else relies solely upon experience, have assurance in things unseen sets an example others will find attractive. Everyone is searching for transcendent meaning in life. Even most atheists look for meaning beyond themselves, a higher directive or mission. (Sometimes that's as simple as the perpetuation of the species.) But we have the answer they're looking for, whether or not their search is conscious. In displaying blind faith, the throngs of people waiting for the next spectacle—be it reality TV, sports, elections, concerts, or whatever—will experience something the basic five senses cannot accommodate: a transcendent glory only God can provide.

Postscript: *When God Says No*

Maybe you have an illness or a disability. Can your faith make you well? Despite our petitions, sometimes God says no because he has a higher purpose we cannot understand. This knowledge doesn't render the pain easy to endure. But here's the deal: if you're afflicted, you'll receive restoration even if it doesn't happen on earth. God will restore all believers in heaven. That might sound like a cop-out, but it's true. Again, that doesn't mean it's easy to have to suffer or endure pain, but these are opportunities for faith on at least two levels. First, we get the opportunity to rely on God to give us what we need to make it day by day. This is why Jesus prayed, "Give us this day, our daily bread" (Matt. 6:11). Learning to trust him for something as basic as bread—something many of us take for granted—is an invaluable lesson. Second, we receive the opportunity to lean on God's promise of restoration, even if it doesn't occur in this life. Knowing what doubting Thomas knew—that Jesus was raised from the dead—should make this type of faith a reasonable thing, but our senses get in the way. We see devastation and destruction and forget about the transcendent nature of God. We forget about the historical fact of the resurrection. Why? Because our senses are so powerful, vibrant, and real. We feel the pain of illness or disability and forget the promise. That pain is unmistakable and cannot be ignored. In these moments when it seems God is saying no, remember that he also said no to Jesus. In the garden, on the cusp of gruesome suffering, Jesus asked God to remove the cup of the cross if he willed.

God said no.

In those moments when our senses can be so stimulating and exciting, it's easy to forget about the transcendent nature of life. It's easy to forget that this earth is temporary. That's why sometimes, as the beggar teaches us, it takes a blind man to really see the truth.

LESSON 8
The Gospel Overcomes Darkness

I do not at all understand the mystery of grace—only that it meets us where we are but does not leave us where it found us.
—Anne Lamott

The Sacred Text

He entered Jericho and was passing through. And behold, there was a man named Zacchaeus. He was a chief tax collector and was rich. And he was seeking to see who Jesus was, but on account of the crowd he could not, because he was small in stature. So he ran on ahead and climbed up into a sycamore tree to see him, for he was about to pass that way. And when Jesus came to the place, he looked up and said to him, "Zacchaeus, hurry and come down, for I must stay at your house today." So he hurried and came down and received him joyfully. And when they saw it, they all grumbled, "He has gone in to be the guest of a man who is a sinner." And Zacchaeus stood and said to the Lord, "Behold, Lord, the half of my goods I give to the poor. And if I have defrauded anyone of anything, I restore it fourfold." And Jesus said to him, "Today salvation has come to this house, since he also is a son of Abraham. For the Son of Man came to seek and to save the lost."

—Luke 19:1–10

In old Jericho, one man's faith in Jesus led to extraordinary healing when Jesus restored sight to Bartimaeus. Now in new Jericho, Jesus would demonstrate the transformative power of his grace. Those considered the farthest from God, those who are the most despicable, and those who seem to be lost causes are never out of reach of God's grace.

Zacchaeus, Sinner

Among the people of Jericho, chief tax collector Zacchaeus would have qualified for superlatives of his own. Among them: least likely to give you a fair deal, most likely to be called "wee little man" by millions of Sunday school kids, and least likely to be accepted by God. But as we know, other than Wee Man, none of those monikers stuck. Jesus sought out Zacchaeus, and despite the tax collector's checkered past, he pledged to offer restitution to those he had wronged. In response, Jesus said, "Today salvation has come to this house, since he also is a son of Abraham" (Luke 19:10).

Don't you love reversal stories like this one? Luke deliberately highlighted these stories, especially in the narrative of Jesus's journey to Jerusalem. We saw it in the previous chapter in the form of a blind beggar whom Jesus healed, and here we have a mob boss who committed to leaving behind a life of corruption. Luke, by the way, is the only gospel writer to include the story of Zacchaeus—exhibit A in a myriad of stories highlighting the Lord's focus on pursuing those gone astray. Or, as Jesus himself said, "The Son of Man came to seek and to save the lost" (Luke 19:10).

And boy was Zacchaeus lost. His name means "pure," a most unfitting name for a dirty-dealing, rotten scoundrel of a Jew. For a people steeped in obsession with ritual cleanliness, Zacchaeus found himself soiled by the sins of greed and exploitation. As a tax collector, he was in a special category of sinner, a profession often singled out for all the vile it represented to the Jews. Tax collectors were known to extract more money than required and keep the extra for themselves. This is why, when tax collectors repented at the preaching of John the Baptist, John advised, "Collect no more than you are authorized to do" (Luke 3:13). When embraced by Jesus, Zacchaeus repented and vowed to restore fourfold if there was anyone he had defrauded. The implication is not that he was unsure or unaware if he had ripped anyone off, but rather the list of victims was so long he couldn't even remember them. But even if Zacchaeus's collections had been on the up-and-up—adhering to John's advice to collect only what was required—he still would have been considered a traitor, a man complicit in the occupation and adulteration of Jerusalem. This explains the reaction of the onlookers who grumbled, muttering that Jesus was going to a sinner's house. But Zacchaeus was no ordinary tax collector; he was the chief tax collector in new Jericho—the lavish Herod-built district of Jericho reserved for the sophisticated upper crust.

Countless throngs of people passed through this city. Just as Jesus and his disciples did, those traveling to Jerusalem (from either the north or the south) typically passed through Jericho, especially during festival seasons like Passover. But Jews weren't the only ones traveling through Jericho. The city lies in the Jordan Rift Valley, which comprises a good chunk of a trade route called the King's Highway, an ancient route connecting Egypt to Mesopotamia. This stretch originates near present-day Cairo and heads due east through the Sinai Peninsula to the Gulf of Aqaba, the northernmost point of the Red Sea. From there, the path turns north, running through the valley all the way to Damascus in Syria until it veers east once again. It's hard to overstate the popularity of the King's Highway in the first century.

Throughout antiquity, dating as far back as Abraham, empires fought for control of this strategic stretch of land. He who held the deed to the King's Highway had an advantage over surrounding nations. So controlling the King's Highway was, in part, what made Herod the Great so great. Under the authority of Rome, he controlled the trade routes across all Israel, which guaranteed him riches and power. Jericho was a key stop along the route. Most of the goods destined for Rome or Corinth from Asia (and vice versa) had to pass through Jericho.[49] You name it: silk, spices, salt, furniture, jewelry, and many other goods passed through Israel.

And guess what the Romans did to all of these merchants traveling along the trade route? They taxed them, of course! After all, the route was safe, secure, and well maintained. Just as with modern toll roads and highways, taxes kept the highway in service. Of course, pilgrims like Jesus and the Twelve found themselves caught up in the racket as well. Everyone passing through had to pay the toll.

Of this massive undertaking, Zacchaeus was in charge. Sure, a Roman commander led a garrison of soldiers in Jericho to keep the peace, but Zacchaeus did all of the dirty work. As chief tax collector, he managed many other tax collectors under him. He trained new recruits and cut free those who didn't meet their quota. He told the lower ranking soldiers whom to shake down and threaten. I can just imagine Zacchaeus holding morning meetings with his lower level tax collectors like a modern telemarketing scheme. "Today is going to be a great day, team! We're gonna rob these people blind. Every man has to reach this quota today. Go get 'em!"

As a representative of Rome, Zacchaeus commanded fear and respect. He may have been short, but he was powerful. He filled the

---

[49] Craig S. Keener, *The IVP Bible Background Commentary: New Testament, 2nd Edition* (Downer's Grove, IL: InterVarsity Press, 2014), 240.

coffers of Rome after all and the name of the game was to extort as much money as possible from each merchant, pilgrim, and traveler. Call it legalized racketeering. After Rome got paid, the remainder went to the Roman commander, then Zacchaeus, and then the tax collectors. The more a tax collector could extract from people, the more he got paid. It was a lucrative operation. As such, Zacchaeus wasn't just powerful—he was filthy rich too. He lived in one of the nicest homes in Herodian Jericho. He rode a brand-new camel with low miles and had the finest clothes. His kids went to the best schools, his wife led the local rotary club, and they had servants who cleaned their home.

Though Zacchaeus may have had friends in high places, the average Jew hated him. He was a "son of Abraham," but he ripped off his own people, and he was colluding with the enemy—Rome. The people considered Zacchaeus scum. They were kind of right. More significantly, they believed the tax collector was beyond the reach of God's love, acceptance, and grace. Jesus, though, saw something in Zacchaeus no one else could see.

Ripe for the Picking

On the day the Lord passed through new Jericho, excitement filled the air. I'm sure it was business as usual in the tax-collecting booth. With Passover close at hand, Jericho was flooded with Jews making their yearly pilgrimage to the city of David. Besides the normal holy day hubbub, Jericho was no doubt in a frenzy by what had just occurred in the life of Bartimaeus, the well-known, once-blind beggar. So as Jesus inched nearer to new Jericho, flanked by throngs of people, anticipation was almost palpable. Were you to reach out your hand, you might feel the electricity pulsing through the breeze. "He has to be the Messiah!" one person shouts. "I wonder what he will do in Jerusalem?" another asks. "Look at Bartimaeus! He can see!"

Count Zacchaeus among those dying to get a glimpse of Jesus. But he didn't just want to see Jesus; Luke tells us he wanted to "see who Jesus was" (Luke 19:3). He wanted to know if Jesus really was a healer, if he really could be the Messiah, if he was indeed a rabbi with authority. As in any good story, our protagonist faced an obstacle to what he desired. He was small in stature, and therefore unable to lay eyes on Jesus since, again, the Lord was surrounded by people. At this point, Zacchaeus had to make a choice. He had to decide if he would do whatever it took to see who this Jesus guy was or head back to the booth to squeeze more cash from travelers. Climbing a tree seemed to be the only viable option in a pinch, but a man of Zacchaeus's standing was not supposed to subject himself to such a humiliating feat. Children climb trees, not sophisticated businessmen. Had Zacchaeus been given advance word that a celebrity would be passing by, he could've gathered his goons to carve out prime real estate near the road. There was no time or means to accomplish such a feat in such a short and unexpected amount of time. So instead, Zacchaeus humiliated himself. He climbed a tree. What a strange sight it was to see a community leader—one feared by the people—in a tree.

Remember the parable about the tax collector in the temple? Zacchaeus displayed all of the characteristics of humility Jesus described in Luke 18:13–14. He humbled himself and sought after Jesus. This was his first step of faith. Sinners must come to Jesus on their knees, humbly aware of their need for Jesus. Zacchaeus was there; therefore, Zacchaeus was ripe for the picking as he rested in the tree! Earlier, Jesus told his disciples, "The harvest is plentiful, but the laborers are few" (Luke 10:2). This of course was a metaphor for those ready to hear and respond to the word. And as Jesus passed by, where was Zacchaeus? Up in a tree—just like a ripe fig ready to be plucked from the branch. All he needed was a laborer to reap the harvest. So when Jesus called the wee man down from the tree, the scripture tells us he "received [Jesus] joyfully" (Luke 19:6).

The Hatchet Man

When we read stories like this, it can be difficult for us to conceptualize their magnitude. Being two millennia removed from the events, they might seem unreal or impossible to relate to. Also, we might be tempted to compartmentalize the stories in the Bible and relegate them to a different sphere of reality. As such, one might believe transformations like that of the tax collector don't occur anymore, but the reality is that the power of the gospel can transform any life at any time. These conversions happen every day all over the world, and you will never hear about most of them because the recipients of grace aren't famous or well publicized, as was the case with Zacchaeus.

But one modern example you may have heard about is that of Charles Wendell Colson. One day in 1973, Chuck, as he was known, gave his life to Christ. Yet because of Colson's reputation as a scoundrel and the circumstances surrounding the event, the world doubted his sincerity.

It's hard to fault those who were skeptical. As special counsel to President Nixon, he had acquired a reputation for barbarous and vindictive behavior, and his willingness to do just about anything to destroy the president's opponents earned him the nickname "Hatchet Man." Colson had other nicknames too. Nixon's chief of staff, H. R. Haldeman, called Colson "the president's personal hit man,"⁵⁰ and *Slate Magazine* described him as an "evil genius."⁵¹ One US senator's staffer joked that Mr. Colson would run over his own grandmother if necessary to accomplish his goals. Though Colson at first distanced himself from the one-liner (both of his grandmothers had been dead for over two decades),⁵² the statement stuck in large part because of the man's ruthless reputation.

Colson's most famous hit job was his campaign against Pentagon Papers leaker Daniel Ellsberg. The Pentagon Papers contained classified information regarding the US strategy and involvement in Vietnam. While employed by the secretary of defense, Robert McNamara, Ellsberg secretly copied the documents as his opinion turned against the war. Viewed as a traitor not only of the Nixon administration but also of America, Colson and his staff sought to discredit and defame Ellsberg in any way possible. The Hatchet Man provided damaging information about Ellsberg's lawyer to the press and prompted a public investigation of Ellsberg's motives and associates.⁵³

But even allies were not immune to Colson's attacks. Enter Federal Reserve Board chairman and longtime friend of Nixon, Arthur Burns. With the economy in rough shape, word from the White House was that recovery was imminent. Burns disagreed. He testified to congress that he was not optimistic about the US economy—the president's policies were preventing recovery. In

---

[50] H. R. Haldeman and Joseph DiMona, *The Ends of Power* (New York: Times Books, 1978), 5.
[51] David Plotz, "Charles Colson: How a Watergate Crook Became America's Greatest Christian Conservative," *Slate*, March 10, 2000, http://www.slate.com/articles/news_and_politics/assessment/2000/03/charles_colson.html.
[52] Charles W. Colson, *Born Again* (Old Tappan, New Jersey: Chosen Books, 1976), 72.
[53] Ibid., 60.

response, Colson leaked to the press the half-truth that Burns was attempting to implement a pay raise for himself.

While not directly involved with—or even aware of—the break-in at the Watergate office complex on June 17, 1972, the heat slowly increased on just about everyone in the Nixon administration, not the least of which was Colson. Nixon's reelection campaign succeeded—he won the 1972 election over George McGovern by one of the biggest margins in the history of the United States. But what started as an ill-advised robbery against political opponents soon ballooned into a scandal of grand scale.

Against this backdrop, Colson's born-again experience seemed like a convenient way to win sympathy from the public—another one of his political tricks. The maneuver looked like classic Colson, one of the shiftiest and shrewdest politicians on the planet. News publications across the country expressed incredulity at the timely conversion. One writer for the *New York Times* went as far to write, "Charles Colson's religious conversion guaranteed a laugh from the grimmest gathering of political sophisticates . . . tinged, nevertheless, by a slight underglow of professional appreciation for what appears to me a supreme con."[54] Even his own law partner, David Shapiro, was incredulous. In a rage, he told Colson, "[Your conversion] looks like the biggest 'dirty trick' you've ever pulled, the final big play for sympathy. It probably is."[55]

Those skeptics, though, never bothered to consult Tom L. Phillips. Mr. Phillips was CEO at Raytheon Company, a weapons and electronics manufacturer. Had the scoffers asked the CEO, they would have understood Colson's transformation was genuine. Why?

---

[54] Richard Goodwin, "The Mask of State," *New York Times*, June 30, 1974, http://www.nytimes.com/books/00/03/26/specials/mccarthy-watergate.html.
[55] Colson, 169–170.

Tom was the man who introduced Colson to Christ. Tom himself was a recent convert, having attended a Billy Graham event in New York out of curiosity.[56] Upon seeing his old acquaintance, Tom could sense something wasn't right with Colson and offered to talk to him about his newfound faith in Christ. "I'd like to tell you the whole story someday, Chuck," he said.[57]

Five months later, he did just that. Colson, feeling the heat from authorities and the stress of Watergate pressing upon him, visited the Phillipses' home. Tom shared his faith with Colson and gave him a copy of the book, *Mere Christianity*, by C. S. Lewis. Less than a week later, Colson surrendered his life to Christ, and eventually to authorities. He pled guilty to obstruction of justice in the Ellsberg trial and spent seven months incarcerated for his crime.

Colson has admitted C. S. Lewis's description of pride in *Mere Christianity* portrayed him to a tee.[58] In another Lewis book, *Surprised by Joy*, Lewis called himself the most reluctant convert in all of England.[59] If that's the case, it might be fair to call Colson the most unlikely convert in the United States of America.

The lesson for the disciples and for us is clear: don't count out the unlikely candidates for the kingdom. This is exactly why Jesus showed up to this earth: to seek out and rescue sinners. What if Jesus had looked the other way when passing Zacchaeus? What if Tom Phillips decided Chuck Colson was too corrupt, too far from God to turn to Christ? Could God have used someone else to present the gospel to Colson? Absolutely. He's God. But he wanted to use Mr. Phillips just like he wants to use you, right where you are. Like Jesus

---

[56] Ibid., 110.
[57] Ibid., 93.
[58] Ibid., 114.
[59] C. S. Lewis, *Surprised by Joy: The Shape of My Early Life* (New York: Harcourt Brace & Co., 1955), 221.

said, the fields are filled with crops ready for harvest, but the laborers are few. Our responsibility is to spread the message to the world. You and I are not responsible for the result; we are simply called to be active in sharing the message of the cross.

The Lord is like a lifeguard scouring the waters for those in peril. He is calling you and me to be a part of this miraculous endeavor. He's calling us to trust him enough to get serious about reaching people. Yes, this includes people we think will never come to know the Lord. Do you know an atheist? How about a drunk or a womanizer? Salvation can come even to the most immoral or vile person you know by the convicting power of the Holy Spirit.

The Least Likely Way to Beat Back Evil

But what does any of this have to do with overcoming evil in the world? How does this empower us to make a difference? This and numerous other gospel lessons teach us that the best way to beat back evil is through personal conviction and conversion. The Spirit prepares hearts and minds to be receptive to Jesus; we must seek those out.

Does that sound off? Does it sound unsatisfying? Maybe. It does to me even as I write this. But think about it for a minute. Jesus came in a way no one expected. Even John the Baptist, who was in tune with the Spirit and had divine ordination from birth, got confused when he found himself a prisoner in Herod's jail. Why was he in prison if Jesus was the Messiah? Why was Herod and his evil reign flourishing? We ask similar questions today. Why is there so much suffering and oppression in the world if God is in charge? The Jews expected Jesus to conquer Rome with a sword. That didn't happen. He would conquer Rome, but it was through the message of his resurrection and through the power of grace and love that he conquered. Over three hundred years after Christ's death, Christianity became the official religion of the Roman Empire. This is so counterintuitive to the way most of us think. Who on earth would arrange for the Son of God to be born to a teenage virgin in a feeding trough? Who would expect him to labor for years as a carpenter? Who would expect him to strip naked and wash his own disciples' feet as if he were a slave? And who, in their right minds, would script a Savior to die in the most humiliating way possible? None of these things make sense, and this kind of disconnect fueled the remarks of the chief priests, scribes, and elders at Jesus's crucifixion where they sneered, "He saved others; he cannot save himself. He is the King of Israel; let him come down now from the cross, and we will believe in him" (Matt. 27:42).

In the same way, personal conviction and conversion can topple nations, transform organizations, and overcome evil. Let's use Billy Graham as an example. What if no one had presented the gospel to him? Countless people may never have turned to God for forgiveness. Chuck Colson wouldn't have done so. Tom Phillips committed his life to Christ because he attended a Graham rally. And later on, it was Tom who presented the gospel to Colson. In response, not only did Colson repent of his former life, but also helped restore many others through his ministry to inmates around the country. Again, God can use any person at any time to present the word, but he wants to use you. Don't underestimate the importance your proactivity in leading others to Christ can have on the kingdom. Walking in faith means sowing seeds and harvesting the crops ready for picking. Think that's hard? The Spirit does all of the hard work. Which is easier? Picking fruit or converting a seed into fruit?

Zacchaeus displayed faith, as we will see, and faith is always the condition of transformation. This high-level tax collector typifies the darkness that still plagues our world today. He was greedy. He cheated people. He was full of corruption and materialism. His sin was not in his wealth per se but rather in how he *accumulated* his wealth. Zacchaeus would step over anyone and everyone—even his own grandmother—to rise to the ranks of the system and get paid. Money was his god and people were a means to his selfish end. Simply put, God was at the very back burner of his life. This self-centered attitude and many other vices are what have plagued humanity for millennia. Today, traditional Judeo-Christian values are ridiculed and rejected in the public square while humanism advances. In the West, birth rates are down but abortions are up. Politics and governments are as corrupt as ever while human suffering increases. Infidelity, cohabitation, and every sort of sexual perversion are on the rise while marriage, purity, and commitment are on the decline. Families are dysfunctional and dysfunction is considered normal, even celebrated.

None of this is new. Human depravity has persisted in varying degrees ever since Cain slaughtered his brother in a jealous rage. Is there any hope? No, not in humanity itself. No amount of discipline, meditation, or random acts of kindness can overcome the sin nature imbedded in mankind. The only hope to overcome a life surrounded by self-centered, idol-loving darkness is a transformational encounter with the Son of God. Faith is the key that unlocks this new God-centered life. Do you want to change the culture? The best way—perhaps the only way—is when one flees darkness and steps into the light of Christ. Doing so requires faith, but you, the Christ follower, must also exercise faith to reap the great evangelistic harvest before you.

Divine Stirring

Every conversion story begins with a call. This can take on many forms. In the case of Zacchaeus, Jesus called him directly. He spotted the man in the tree, recognized his faith, and declared he had to stay at Zacchaeus's home. This wasn't a rude self-invite, but rather Christ was explaining that he and Zacchaeus had a divine appointment—Jesus had marching orders from the Father to meet with Zacchaeus. The Lord took notice of the tax collector's humility and called after him.

In a similar manner, Jesus calls all sinners to come to him. He calls people to drop their old way of life and enter into the light he offers. Although he's no longer on earth in physical form—through the proclamation of the Gospel and the activity of the Holy Spirit to draw, convict, and convince—Jesus is still scheduling divine appointments with people today. He's still calling people to leave darkness and become disciples. And he's using the church like an instrument in the hands of a virtuoso to send out his message. Whether it's a pastor on stage Sunday morning, a group of college students evangelizing a beach during spring break, or a grandmother teaching songs to children at VBS, Jesus is using the church for divine appointments. Jesus is leveraging the faith quotient of believers to bring about faith in lost people. So you could say that faith begets faith. In Jericho, Jesus picked the fruit from the tree himself by calling the tax collector. Guess who was watching? Twelve weary disciples who had a front-row seat to faith episode after faith episode. Were they willing to follow the example of the rabbi? Are we eager to be a part of the great evangelistic harvest?

What's the point? To be an instrument in the hands of Jesus and advance the kingdom—to transform culture by leading someone out of darkness—you must have eager faith. You must be willing to be used of God! Jesus wants to use you for divine appointments. Are you following him? Jesus uses people like you to share the good news. Are you eager to share? Jesus can use your story to lead people to him. Are you engaging and investing in people?

Jesus invested in Zacchaeus, and the yield was incredible. Who would have thought such a corrupt man could find redemption? And yet the tax collector trusted in Jesus, receiving him "joyfully" (Luke 19:6). This word is translated from the Greek *chairo*, meaning "to be cheerful." In the King James, the word here is *rejoicing*. So in using *chairo*, Luke goes beyond mere hospitality, wishing to express Zacchaeus's inner joy. This isn't a superficial reception. Zacchaeus didn't just open his home to Jesus, but also his heart. He, too, was enthusiastically eager. Just as with Chuck Colson, when a person receives acceptance and forgiveness from God, some pretty remarkable things begin to happen in that person's heart. Zacchaeus was no exception.

In context, it appears that after dismounting the sycamore, Zacchaeus hosted a traditional Jewish dinner party for Jesus; it was customary for distinguished community members to host famous rabbis or other important figures. These soirees were public affairs. Only invitees could eat at the table, but anyone could gather and observe the spectacle. The onlookers, though intrigued, scoffed at the sight of Jesus hanging out with the likes of Zacchaeus. Again, this goes to show just how rotten of a guy Zacchaeus was, while at the same time giving us yet another glimpse into the real nature of Jesus's ministry. Jesus sought out the wretched and broken. In fact, Zacchaeus probably found himself in good company considering the Twelve were a bunch of misfits too, including a fellow tax collector in Matthew.

Face-to-face with Jesus, Zacchaeus couldn't help but examine his own life and feel conviction. In response, he said, "Behold, Lord, the half of my goods I give to the poor" (Luke 19:8). In typical Jewish fashion, Zacchaeus declared his intentions in front of the whole community so they could hold him accountable. This was equivalent to a legal decree—Zacchaeus was serious about his decision to follow Jesus. Half of his possessions was no small sum for a chief tax collector in a major trade city. But Zacchaeus didn't stop there. He said, "And if I have defrauded anyone of anything, I restore it fourfold." Zacchaeus likely used Exodus 22:1 as his basis for pledging fourfold restoration: "If a man steals an ox or a sheep, and kills it or sells it, he shall repay five oxen for an ox, and four sheep for a sheep." This is a picture of real transformation. Zacchaeus was not interested in half-heartedly following the Messiah. He was all in. And Jesus said salvation came that very day.

Stories like this and Colson's are amazing, but when a person experiences salvation, this sort of transformation is the norm, not the exception. And God often uses his people to initiate the transaction. Jesus demonstrated faithfulness in calling Zacchaeus down from the tree. Tom Phillips simply told Chuck Colson his own story of transformation. Our point is that faith in the face of evil need not always be grandiose or heroic. It means relying upon God to reveal to you the actions you need to take. It means saying yes when he calls. God will take care of the hard part; you must be ready and willing to accept the challenge when the time comes. Christ works to combat evil by internal transformation, one heart at a time. Although it may seem inefficient, it is undoubtedly effective.

LESSON 9
Faith Always Produces Action

To live in chronic fear extracts the highest cost of all.[60]
—John Ortberg

The Sacred Text

As they heard these things, he proceeded to tell a parable, because he was near to Jerusalem, and because they supposed that the kingdom of God was to appear immediately. He said therefore, "A nobleman went into a far country to receive for himself a kingdom and then return. Calling ten of his servants, he gave them ten minas, and said to them, 'Engage in business until I come.' But his citizens hated him and sent a delegation after him, saying, 'We do not want this man to reign over us.' When he returned, having received the kingdom, he ordered these servants to whom he had given the money to be called to him, that he might know what they had gained by doing business. The first came before him, saying, 'Lord, your mina has made ten minas more.' And he said to him, 'Well done, good servant! Because you have been faithful in a very little, you shall have authority over ten cities.' And the second came, saying, 'Lord, your mina has made five minas.' And he said to him,

---

[60] John Ortberg, *If You Want to Walk on Water, You've Got to Get Out of the Boat* (Waterville, ME: Thorndike Press, 2003), 230.

'And you are to be over five cities.' Then another came, saying, 'Lord, here is your mina, which I kept laid away in a handkerchief; for I was afraid of you, because you are a severe man. You take what you did not deposit, and reap what you did not sow.' He said to him, 'I will condemn you with your own words, you wicked servant! You knew that I was a severe man, taking what I did not deposit and reaping what I did not sow? Why then did you not put my money in the bank, and at my coming I might have collected it with interest?' And he said to those who stood by, 'Take the mina from him, and give it to the one who has the ten minas.' And they said to him, 'Lord, he has ten minas!' 'I tell you that to everyone who has, more will be given, but from the one who has not, even what he has will be taken away. But as for these enemies of mine, who did not want me to reign over them, bring them here and slaughter them before me.'"

—Luke 19:11–27

How would you live if you knew the world was going to end three weeks from Saturday? You'd probably stop worrying about your diet. You might stop going to work. And I can just about guarantee you're not going to floss. Why would it matter? Everything's over in less than a month anyway.

Neighbors Dodge and Penny in the film *Seeking a Friend for the End of the World* face this very scenario. A seventy-mile-wide asteroid nicknamed Matilda is approaching Earth, and all attempts to divert it have failed. Matilda will collide with Earth in twenty-one days. In response, the world goes crazy. Several people commit suicide. Some people prefer denial, still showing up to work or running on the treadmill at the gym. But the majority of humanity embraces all the vices from which it used to abstain when, you know, the world wasn't going to blow up. Alcohol, drugs, and sex rule the day. There's no tomorrow, and humanity lives like it.

As for me? If the world is about to end, I'm eating doughnuts for dinner. I'm calling the house painter and telling him, "Never mind." I'm stopping investments in my Roth IRA. In fact, I'd probably cash out all of my bank accounts and investments—assuming money was still worth anything. And I'd stop writing on my blog, stop writing my next book. What's the point?

If you can relate to this mind-set, then you can understand the prophet Jeremiah's confusion when God instructed him to buy his cousin's field as the Babylonians were about to sack Jerusalem. Imagine your state overrun by invaders who came to drag you away to another land, but just before you go, you call up your realtor and tell him or her you want to purchase your nephew's condo. What does it matter? You're about to be invaded and exiled! In dismay, Jeremiah asks God what's going on:

> Behold, the siege mounds have come up to the city to take it, and because of sword and famine and pestilence the city is given into the hands of the Chaldeans who are fighting against it. What you spoke has come to pass, and behold, you see it. Yet you, O LORD GOD, have said to me, "Buy the field for money and get witnesses"—though the city is given into the hands of the Chaldeans."
> —Jeremiah 32:24–25

Jeremiah couldn't imagine why on earth he should have to spend his hard-earned shekels on a piece of land that would belong to the Chaldeans in a matter of days. Israel's world, from the human perspective, was coming to an end. There was no tomorrow for Judah—at least not one that was any good. Even the prophet didn't know what future God had in store for his people. It may have seemed like the end of the world, but God had other plans. God used this real estate transaction as a demonstration to Jeremiah and Judah that he would restore the people. God asked his prophet to step out on faith and purchase a worthless plot of land. He told Jeremiah to plan for the long haul.

There's a similar dynamic going on as Jesus approached Jerusalem for the last time. According to Luke's gospel, Jesus told the Parable of the Minas because the people believed the kingdom of God would come at once.

> He proceeded to tell a parable, because he was near to Jerusalem, and because they supposed that the kingdom of God was to appear immediately.
> —Luke 19:11

Of course, the crowds around Jesus couldn't comprehend the gravity of God's kingdom. They expected a kingdom like David's that would overthrow Israel's oppressors and restore its freedom. So while the Jews didn't think the world was coming to an end, they did believe Jesus's kingdom would be established on earth when he reached Jerusalem.

Therefore, Jesus related the Parable of the Minas to his followers as a demonstration that kingdom work is not done. In the story, a nobleman goes away to another country to receive a kingdom and return. Before he leaves, he calls up ten of his servants and grants them each a mina (about three months' wages). Then the master says to the servants, "Engage in business until I come." The New International Version reads, "Put this money to work . . . until I come back" (Luke 19:13).

This command is essential to the parable. Do you see what Jesus was trying to tell the people? First, he attempted to prepare them for his absence. Second, he wanted them to know there is work still to be done. Jesus knew if we thought he was coming tomorrow or in three weeks, we'd stop working.

In Lesson 1, we talked about the privilege of living between revelations of Jesus. We weren't here for his first coming, but we have record of it; therefore, we have assurance of salvation and hope of his return. But that also means we have more responsibility. God requires action in proportion to revelation. We know Jesus came, died, and rose from the grave just as he said he would, but that was just the beginning. Now that Jesus has provided a way by which humanity can be saved—through his atoning death—we must spread the gospel to those who aren't aware.

The Bible reinforces the tilt toward action after Jesus rose from the dead. One example is the Great Commission, the mission statement Jesus gave to his disciples: "Go therefore and make disciples of all nations" (Matt. 28:19b). Another example is the scene in which Jesus ascended into heaven. The disciples stood in amazement, necks craned and staring into the sky with slack jaws and wonder in their hearts. After some time, two men in white (presumably angels) reminded them to get back to work: "Men of Galilee, why do you stand looking into heaven? This Jesus, who was taken up from you into heaven, will come in the same way as you saw him go into heaven" (Acts 1:11). Just before his ascension, Jesus told the disciples they would be his witnesses throughout the earth (1:8). The angels reminded them that Jesus is coming back, but the meantime is no time to stand around. There's work to be done! No one knows the day or the hour God has set for Christ's return. Until then, we must use what gifts he has given us, multiplying them for the benefit of the King and his kingdom.

What the Faithful Know That the Fearful Don't

Thinking of investing for retirement causes some people to seize up in fear. Even diversified portfolios filled with mutual funds scare some people out of the investing business altogether. Questions nag them at night while dressed in their flannel pajamas and lying between their flannel sheets: *What if I lost it all? What if the market dives when I need the money?*

When it comes to investing cash, nothing worthwhile completely eliminates risk. No one knew this better than the unfaithful servant who clutched his mina. What did he do? Rather than risk losing the money, he wrapped the dough in a hanky and handed it back to the master, untouched, upon his return. The master was not impressed. In fact, he condemned the fearful man, calling him a "wicked servant" (Luke 19:22).

The man's visceral fear is not uncommon; we can all relate to avoiding risk in some form or another.

When my wife and I (Andrew) sold our first home and bought another, pretty much everything that could have gone wrong did. Our first buyers got cold feet and backed out. Once we finalized a contract with another buyer, we thought we were home free. Selling is the hard part, right? Shopping for a new home started out fun and exciting, then turned to grueling and laborious. When we finally decided on a home to purchase and settled on a price, we booked one of those double closing days: sell in the morning, then buy in the afternoon. What could possibly go wrong? "People do it every day," our black-haired, over-pomped realtor assured us.

The selling went okay, though not without some drama. (Seriously, this whole ordeal could be a miniseries on Telemundo.) While closing on the house we were selling, we had to sign a dozen forms. That done, a woman handed us a check from the proceeds of the sale. It was a six-figure check. The plan was to tuck the neat little piece of paper into a fancy white envelope for a couple of hours, then use it as a down payment on our new home, which we would be closing on later that afternoon.

If only it were that easy.

Closing on the home we were buying was delayed. Our financing wasn't ready.

We were now responsible for safeguarding this piece of paper representing our entire net worth until we bought the new house. "What do I do with this check?" I asked our realtor. I expected him to say he had some super-secret vault impervious to fire and thieves and nuclear weaponry. His response was far less satisfying. "Hang on to it until we close on your new house."

Through incompetence and mistakes, the closing didn't happen for almost three weeks. *Three weeks.* For nearly a month, we sat on this check. I lay in bed thinking, *I wonder where that check is?* even though I knew good and well it was tucked into an oversized folder and resting on a shelf in my master closet. *I'll just get up and check to make sure it's still there.* Wash. Rinse. Repeat. I was tempted to cash it and fill a briefcase with the money. (I've always wanted to do that.) I could use a few of those dollars to buy some handcuffs, and Katie and I could take turns handcuffing the briefcase to our wrists, like it contained nuclear launch codes.

One thing about the Parable of the Minas we might miss is the sum of money involved. A mina is about three months' salary. I don't know about you, but that's a lot of money to me. Reading the story in Luke, it's easy to assume we're dealing with only a hundred bucks. Regardless of the amount, the servant disobeyed his master. Before he left, the master said, "Engage in business until I come" (Luke 19:13). Hiding the money away in a handkerchief is kind of the opposite of that. The servant disobeyed not out of malice but out of fear of loss. But do you think the two faithful servants didn't have fears? They did. However, rather than allow worry to paralyze them, they proceeded on faith. They feared (read: revered) their master more than they feared losing $10,000. So they got to work.

That's the thing about living by faith: it's risky. What if you pour everything you have—your money, time, talents, effort—into a ministry or a soul and you fail? What if you lose it all? Even if these fears are legitimate and validated, faith often involves acting on what God tells us to do without knowing how things will turn out. Whether you're faithful or fearful doesn't change that fact. Only God knows the outcome of our decisions and our lives. But what the faithful know that the fearful don't is this: risk is unavoidable.

It's like a man who spends his whole life trying to avoid risk only to get cancer and die within a month of his diagnosis. He couldn't have done anything to prevent (or predict) the illness. Rather than run from risk, why not embrace it? If God is asking you to do something, he won't leave you high and dry to figure it out on your own.

When God told Abram he would beget innumerable offspring, Abram believed. And Scripture tells us that God "counted it to him as righteousness" (Gen. 15:6). Abram was old. His wife was old. Yet God promised him a multitude of descendants. None of that made sense, but still Abram believed. When Sarah finally gave birth to Isaac, God tested the faith of Abram, now called Abraham, by asking him to sacrifice his own son.

Rahab risked her neck to house the Israelite spies. As a result, she survived the onslaught of Israel and became part of the lineage of Jesus. Shadrach, Meshach, and Abednego didn't know if they'd survive the furnace, but they acted on faith and refused to bow to Nebuchadnezzar's golden image. Many more stories like these line the pages of the Bible. Ordinary people believed God and obeyed him despite the risks of doing so. Hebrews 11:6 tells us that "without faith it is impossible to please [God]." I don't know about you, but I'll take that over temporary safety any day.

The Riskiest Thing You Can Do with Your Gifts

Risk is inevitable, but employing our resources for the kingdom isn't all that perilous compared to the alternative. In fact, the riskiest thing you can do with your gifts is to do nothing with them at all.

I used to work with a man named Charlie who didn't trust banks. He was a good guy, always sidling up to you with a sheepish grin and a new story to tell. He chain-smoked too, and he liked to wear an old green jacket. I didn't question him on the bank thing, but I wonder about it sometimes. I imagine him collecting his paycheck and then visiting the Wright's IGA supermarket where a woman with a too-tight bun exchanges Charlie's endorsement for little rectangular stacks of green paper. When Charlie got home, where did he store his money? Did he save for retirement? If he doesn't trust banks, I doubt a cookie jar would suffice. Maybe he buries it in his backyard.

A mild distrust of banks is healthy, if you ask me, but burying your money—as the unfaithful servant found out—is worse than trusting a bank. Even if you never touch the money again, depositing it in a bank account will at least earn you some interest. But thanks to inflation, stashing money in a shoebox means you are actually losing money. Therefore, cash is a depreciating asset. In this sense, it's either growing or it's losing value.

Consider these numbers. Let's use $10,000 as a round estimate of the mina given to each servant (three months' wages). That may be close to accurate today, but what about fifty years ago? According to the Bureau of Labor Statistic's Consumer Price Inflation calculator,

$10,000 in 2015 had the same buying power as $1,324 in 1965.[61] In other words, if you were given $1,324 in 1965, it had the buying power of $10,000 in 2015. But if you sat on that $1,324 for fifty years? Suddenly, it's not worth so much. What happened? The number of dollars stayed the same, but the worth of each dollar decreased over time. We've all experienced this in some form or another, even from one year to the next. When once we could buy a gallon of milk for $3, within a year's time, that same gallon costs $3.25, $3.50, or more. What about gasoline? Automobiles? Homes? Health insurance? College tuition? While these prices fluctuate, the overall trend is up. Suddenly, that penny isn't worth as much as it once was. So you see, while investing might be risky, it's riskier to do nothing with your money. You're all but guaranteed to lose it.

This isn't true only of money. While inflation may not affect skills or talents, these things will depreciate and deteriorate just like atrophied muscles. I'm a good example of this fact. Between college and high school, I studied Spanish for six years, including a one-month immersion program in Guadalajara, Mexico, toward the end of college. By that time, I was practically fluent. I could read, write, understand, and even speak decent Castellano. Yet after I walked down the stadium bleachers and across the graduation stage, I rarely used the language. Rather than seek out opportunities to use this skill, I wrapped it in a handkerchief and tucked it away. A decade later, I can still read Spanish pretty well, but I'm slow in audible comprehension. As for speaking? Forget about it. You see what happened? I didn't use the skill, and it kindly departed.

The parable doesn't mention how long the master was gone. I imagine it was a long time for the first servant to have been able to

---

[61] "CPI Inflation Calculator," http://www.bls.gov/data/inflation_calculator.htm.

turn one mina into ten. For you and me, that time is now. The master, Jesus, has gone away. In the meantime, he's entrusted to us spiritual gifts and resources—both financial and others—and he expects us to put them to work. This isn't just a matter of obedience; we either use our gifts or lose them. The unfaithful servant still had his mina intact, but because he didn't do anything with the money, the master took it from him and gave it to the faithful servant. He didn't use his gift, and he lost it.

Idleness and fear are not options. Both lead to destitution. The only option is to actively cultivate and employ our resources for the benefit of the master.

Let's take a second to appreciate the big picture of faith. In recording Jesus's trek to Jerusalem, Luke highlighted various episodes and teachings all dealing with matters of faith. It would seem appropriate at this point, right before Jesus and company entered Jerusalem, to include one last lesson. Specifically, Luke highlighted this Parable of the Minas because it deals with the faithfulness of the disciples. They were the ones who would carry the proverbial gospel torch. The onus would be on these men to continue the work that Christ began.

So Jesus began teaching his ragtag crew about the importance of faith and the various roles it plays in different situations. In some ways, faith needs to be like that of a child, and in other ways, it needs to be tenacious like that of a widow who must carry on without her soul mate. For the believer, faith can accomplish the impossible, and for the unbeliever, it's a requirement to be saved and enter the kingdom.

Luke also highlighted interactions with various people in which faith played a critical role in their spiritual development. The leper was an outcast, the tax collector was hated, and the blind man was a burden on society, yet because of their faith, everything changed. The entire trajectory of their earthly and spiritual lives shifted dramatically. Zacchaeus had more in common with the rich young ruler, yet one had faith and gave his possessions away while the other lacked the faith to forsake all of his possessions and follow Jesus. After imparting all of these examples and lessons to the disciples, Jesus then zeroed in on the disciples' commitment after his departure.

Just as with most of the lessons on the road to Jerusalem, faithfulness is the focus of the Parable of the Minas: Jesus will reward faithfulness and will punish neglect. The nobleman represents Jesus. His death, burial, resurrection, and ascension is like the nobleman going away to be crowned. Jesus ascended into heaven to rule and reign at the right hand of the Father. At the throne, the Son received the fullness of the kingdom from God the Father. Having paved the way for construction of the kingdom through his blood, Jesus is now concerned with filling that kingdom with sons and daughters. The Lord's second advent is likened to the nobleman's return. At some point in the future, he will return to earth to call into account the work of his subjects.

The ten servants (the number ten typically represents fullness and completion) represent you and me—everybody who is in Christ, born again through faith. While a mina is a significant sum of money in the story, it represents the gifts, talents, and abilities God has bestowed upon his people. The citizens who despised the nobleman are the Jewish religious leaders who schemed and plotted to have Christ murdered at the hands of the Roman Empire.

When he told the parable, Jesus was still in Jericho but heading to Jerusalem. He told this story to dispel the belief that he would be a political and military Messiah who would overthrow the Romans when he entered Jerusalem. As in a coup, the people imagined the kingdom would appear immediately. So Jesus's intention was to explain that his followers will be responsible for advancing the kingdom after his departure, working as faithful stewards.

No one could understand that Jesus came first to be a suffering Messiah. The disciples and Jewish religious leaders confused the timeline of the Messiah in the Old Testament, and it's hard to blame them. The Old Testament often paints all aspects of the Messiah in one movement and breath. For example, Isaiah 7 not only predicts the virgin birth of Christ, but the prophet also references the coming tribulation after Jesus ascends into heaven. So in just a few passages of prophesy, there's a span of history that stretches thousands of years. Despite their confusion, the disciples believed Jesus, but the religious leaders, in their confusion, rejected and conspired against the Lord out of pride.

While the Master Is Away

I have either good or bad news for you: you will be held accountable for your faithfulness (or lack thereof) to Jesus. If you live like the good steward, you can rest assured Jesus will reward your diligence and attention to detail. On the other hand, if you have neglected your responsibilities to Christ, you will face repercussions. First Corinthians 3:10–15 describes what is typically called the judgment seat of Christ. This is essentially what the Parable of the Minas describes in allegorical form. Jesus will call on every believer throughout history to give an account of what he or she has done for Christ in his absence. We will all have to testify to our faithfulness. Are we being risky and using our gifts for his kingdom? Or are we simply hiding our gifts in a handkerchief? Unfortunately, many Christians do not take the judgment of Christ seriously.

Certainly, this judgment has nothing to do with whether or not a believer will enter into glory. That has already been settled. The believer is saved, and his or her reward is the glory of heaven. Praise

God! Instead, the judgment seat of Christ has everything to do with rewards in the millennial reign as described in Revelation 20:1–6. In the parable, faithfulness with money translated into control over cities in the new kingdom. Likewise, believers will reign with Christ on earth for a thousand years, and their governing responsibility will be directly related to their faithfulness to Christ during the In-Between. Are you living faithfully to Jesus? Are you honoring him with your decisions? Are you holding on to sin? Are you diligently involved in ministry to move the kingdom forward, or are you sitting on the sidelines? Is your faith risky?

I have another bit of news. A lot is at stake. More than you could ever imagine is riding on your faithfulness to Christ. In the parable, the faithful stewards made wise financial gains. Believers are faithful when they make wise spiritual gains regarding the lost. God has entrusted us with the souls of the earth, the lost sheep, and our job is to move the kingdom of God forward. And the kingdom is not an earthly one comprised of portfolios and acquisitions, but, rather, one comprised of people.

I (Daniel) became a Christian as a teenager as a direct result of the faithfulness of another sixteen-year-old kid. Willy was the first true Christian I had ever met. Taking me, the new kid, under his wing could have been social suicide in high school. Thankfully, Willy's devotion to Christ superseded his need for peer approval. Willy shared the good news with me and lived it out daily. He never gave up on me, even though I rejected his gospel time and again. One day, his faithfulness paid off. I turned to Jesus in faith. He took a huge risk!

Willy, in one way or another, played a role in advancing the kingdom of heaven. In that moment, he was faithful. In hindsight, a lot was riding on Willy's faithfulness. What if he didn't want to take on the new kid? What if he ignored the Spirit's nudging on his heart?

What if Willy had been caught up in some sin and was tuning out God's voice? What if he *didn't* risk it all? I'm pretty thankful Willy was tracking with the Lord.

What about you? Who has God placed in your path? You may be the only person who can reach that someone with the gospel. I hope you're willing to be a faithful servant, wisely investing your minas while the King is away, because you know someone like I was who's counting on it. That all sounds great on paper, but what about in your life? Let me offer some practical keys to having risky faith. First, you have to *leverage* your spiritual gifts, talents, and abilities for the kingdom. What are you good at? What are your passions? Why not use those things for God's glory?

How has God gifted you? As a believer, the Spirit of God has given you at least one gift to be used for ministry. Is it teaching or preaching? Is it evangelism or hospitality? Whatever it is, you have a spiritual gift, and I hope you're using it rather than burying it in the ground.

What about your talents? Can you sing? Are you artistic? Can you shred a guitar? The church needs talented people who will use their God-given gifts for him.

What are your abilities? Are you the sort of person who has a knack for turning a quarter into a hundred dollars? Are you a people person? Use these abilities to advance the kingdom—or fund it!

Dr. K is a member of a church where I was once on staff. He's a family medicine doctor and had the privilege of treating my entire family. Going to Dr. K's office was not a normal trip to the doctor. His waiting area was a Christian library that had books for any topic, ranging from depression to spiritual growth. These were free to anyone who wished to take one. All of his nurses and staff were over the top with excellent bedside manner and politeness. Dr. K was not only a great doctor who would go out of his way to help his patients with science and medicine but he would also witness to, pray with, and spiritually encourage his patients. His godly reputation in the community was well known through word of mouth, as Dr. K lived out what he believed. He leveraged his gifts, talents, and abilities for the kingdom. It doesn't matter what sort of platform you have or what you do for a living. If you follow Jesus, you can leverage your assets for the benefit of the kingdom—but it will take faith.

Second, if you're serious about being faithful and risking it all, you must *stay focused*. We need to live in constant awareness that the King will return with his kingdom. It would have been easy for the stewards in the parable to become lazy as they thought about how long their master would be gone. *Why work so hard now when it could be months or years before he gets back?* Instead, the two faithful servants kept the return of their master in mind. They knew he could return and call them into account at any moment. In the same way, we must keep Jesus's imminent return constantly before us. When we understand he will return without warning and call us into account, we will stay committed to the task and call he has given us.

I have a friend who sensed God's call to do something different with his life. As a successful athlete in college, he had always dreamed of becoming a personal coach and trainer for young men who aspired to play college basketball. So he did what any reasonable person would do. He quit his steady job to devote all of his attention to a business that did not exist. He used his passion and knowledge of basketball to train young men to be better players. Further, he used his spiritual gift of leadership and influence to instill Christian values into mostly inner-city kids who came from rough backgrounds. It wasn't easy. It still isn't easy. He went months without a source of income. He struggled to find clients and to establish a successful business plan. But he didn't quit. He stayed focused on what he believed was God's calling on his life. Things started slow and sometimes barely progressed, but after a while, the hard work and focus paid off. Now he is not only doing what he loves but also is influencing the next generation for Jesus through basketball. His level of focus was admirable and something we all could learn from.

Finally, faithful stewards who risk it all should have a *healthy fear of God*. This may seem strange since Luke 19:21 tells us that the unfaithful servant was the fearful one. But a healthy fear is measured by respect and reverence toward God. The unfaithful servant possessed an ungodly fear, and he used it as his excuse for burying the mina instead of engaging in business as instructed. The nobleman, upon returning, called him on his fear, essentially saying, "If you were so afraid, then you should've gotten busy working!" The truth is that the unfaithful servant wasn't so much afraid of his master finding out he had been lazy as much as he was afraid of failure. He was afraid that he might mess up a transaction or invest in the wrong thing. In contrast, the faithful servants truly did revere their master. They feared him enough that they didn't want to let him down. They respected him enough that they got busy with their investments and business strategies. Their fear motivated them to work hard for their master.

Before my senior year of high school, the football team received an entirely new coaching staff. My junior year, we had only managed one win. It was a depressing year. Week after week, our confidence dwindled with every lopsided loss. However, when Coach McGrew showed up, he brought in a new culture and attitude. Essentially, he commanded respect and his players never took him lightly. He was just the right mix of a caring father and a dangerous grizzly bear. As a result, the entire attitude of the team changed. It was as if every player were playing for the coach. No one wanted to let McGrew down for a lack of effort and feel the scorn of his disappointment. With the same players and a simple change of perspective, a one-win team turned things around and became a playoff team. The only thing that was different was a coach whom the players feared in a healthy way. Because of that fear, respect, and reverence, everyone played harder and fought for victory. The same should be true for us. We should fear the Master enough that we work in diligence to expand his kingdom while he's away.

Instead of living like there's no tomorrow or living in fear of loss, God expects us step out on faith—however risky doing so may seem—and get to work leveraging the gifts at our disposal to grow his kingdom and drive away the darkness in our world. This is as true for you as it was for the disciples who were about to see their rabbi nailed to a cross. With this last lesson of Christ in place, Passion Week could begin.

LESSON 10
Jesus's Death Destroys Darkness

If Christ be not raised, your faith is vain.
I Corinthians 15:17, KJV

The Sacred Text

And taking the twelve, [Jesus] said to them, "See, we are going up to Jerusalem, and everything that is written about the Son of Man by the prophets will be accomplished. For he will be delivered over to the Gentiles and will be mocked and shamefully treated and spit upon. And after flogging him, they will kill him, and on the third day he will rise." But they understood none of these things. This saying was hidden from them, and they did not grasp what was said.

—Luke 18:31–34

The day Roger Bannister ran the first sub-four-minute mile, the wind was too gusty for the runner's liking. He almost canceled the race, assuming conditions had to be perfect to break a record thought unbeatable by many.

Reporting on a contest ran two decades earlier, a writer for the *Southeast Missourian* opined, "The 'four-minute mile' is still a dream. It may come, but it will take an occasion when the pacing as well as the competition is perfectly arranged."[62] In that same year, 1935, US track coach Brutus Hamilton published a list of what he believed were peak possible performances in various events. He called the list *The Ultimate of Human Effort*. His ultimate time for the mile run? 4:01.6.[63] Hamilton did not arrive at these numbers by whim, nor did he rely solely on his expertise as a coach and former track athlete. Instead, he enlisted the help of Finnish physicists to calculate the limits of humankind.[64] It is, perhaps, ironic then that the first man to surpass this "ultimate of human effort," Gunder Hägg, was born just a few hundred miles west of these very physicists in Albacken, Sweden. In 1945, Hägg ran one mile in 4:01.4, two-tenths of a second faster than Hamilton thought possible. But although the coach had been proven wrong, that magical four-minute barrier remained intact. Hägg's record would stand for almost ten years, adding to the mythology of the unbreakability of the four-minute mark. Spectators, sportswriters, and, apparently, some medical professionals thought running one mile in fewer than 240 seconds to be impossible.[65]

But Roger Bannister was a part of the medical field too, a third-year med student at St. Mary's. (He spent the morning before the race rounding on patients.) Clearly, Bannister didn't think the feat

---

[62] "Lovelock Runs Legs off Cunningham, Wins Mile in Easy Shape," *Southeast Missourian* (Cape Girardeau, MO), June 17, 1935.
[63] Neal Bascomb, *The Perfect Mile: Three Athletes, One Goal, and Less Than Four Minutes to Achieve It* (Boston: Houghton Mifflin, 2005), 63.
[64] Frank Litsky, "How Fast? How Far? No Limits in Sight," *New York Times*, June 16, 1986, http://www.nytimes.com/1986/06/16/sports/how-fast-how-far-no-limits-in-sight.html.
[65] Bruce Lowitt, "Bannister Stuns World with 4-Minute Mile," *St. Petersburg Times*, December 17, 1999, http://www.sptimes.com/News/121799/Sports/Bannister_stuns_world.shtml.

impossible or he wouldn't have even attempted it. The myth that one would die if he could accomplish the feat was just that—a myth. More legend than science. In reality, there was nothing magical about the number four, except that the barrier had never been scaled before. Some called it the Everest of the running world. And yet, Sir Edmund Hillary had completed the first ascent up the tallest mountain one year earlier. If Everest could be conquered, certainly someone could run 5,280 feet in 240 seconds. Right?

Bannister sure thought so.

But that wind was brutal.

It was May 6, 1954, a day Bannister had hand-picked. Yet he knew the gusts would cost him precious seconds. Before calling the race off, he decided to wait and see if the weather would calm down. He was so wishy-washy that day, finally his pacesetters demanded, "Come on, Roger, do make up your mind."[66] With what seemed like a lull in the wind, Roger Bannister took the track with Chris Brasher, his first pacesetter.

The gun fired.

False start by Brasher.

The gun fired again, and they were off. Off to make history.

Bannister ran the mile in 03:59:04. He was officially the fastest man in the world.

And yet, within two months, something funny happened. Australian John Landy, just forty-six days after Bannister broke the decade-long record, ran the mile in 3:57.9. Forty-seven days after that, Landy and Bannister both broke the four-minute barrier again in a race at the British Empire and Commonwealth Games in Vancouver. The

---

[66] Roger Bannister, "Roger Bannister: 'The Day I Broke the Four-Minute Mile,'" *The Telegraph*, March 30, 2014, http://www.telegraph.co.uk/sport/10731234/Roger-Bannister-The-day-I-broke-the-four-minute-mile.html.

following year, three runners ran sub-four-minute miles. In 1956, runners accomplished the feat nine times. Within a span of just over two years, athletes had demolished the mythical four-minute barrier sixteen times.[67] That same year—1956—an American named Steve Scott was born. Scott would go on to set the world record for most sub-four-minute miles, accomplishing the feat a staggering 136 times.[68]

Jesus: Buzzkiller

Astute readers like yourself will notice Andrew and I skipped over four verses from Luke 18. This is not to dismiss or discredit the importance of the passage. On the contrary, this is the most critical section of the entire travel narrative. These four verses are the glue that holds the gospel together and upon which one has the ability to express genuine faith. Here's what Luke wrote:

> And taking the twelve, [Jesus] said to them, "See, we are going up to Jerusalem, and everything that is written about the Son of Man by the prophets will be accomplished. For he will be delivered over to the Gentiles and will be mocked and shamefully treated and spit upon. And after flogging him, they will kill him, and on the third day he will rise." But they understood none of these things. This saying was hidden from them, and they did not grasp what was said.
> —Luke 18:31–34

---

[67] Peter Larsson, "All-time Men's Best Mile Race," *Track and Field All-time Performances*, updated November 18, 2017, http://www.alltime-athletics.com/m_mileok.htm.

[68] Daniel P. Smith, "Sub-Four Magic," *Runner's World*, May 6, 2014, https://www.runnersworld.com/elite-runners/sub-four-magic.

The people of Bannister's day assumed he would die trying to run a sub-four mile. He didn't. In contrast, people of the first century believed the Christ would never die. At least not the way Jesus described, at the hands of the filthy Gentiles. If such a travesty occurred, how could he be the Messiah? He was to restore Israel—to snatch it back from the occupying pagans, not suffer at their hands! This is why the disciples "understood none of these things." They could not comprehend a world in which Jesus would suffer in the manner he described. It was simply incompatible with their view of the Christ.

Can you imagine traveling with Jesus, watching him perform miracles and teach the crowds? Jesus fed five thousand men with a few fish and loaves of bread. He taught in a way that left people dumbfounded at his depth, insight, and new revelation. Crowds followed him and marveled. People begged to be near him. Kings feared him. If you were one of the twelve disciples, it meant that Jesus had called you out of an ordinary life, and you had the privilege to watch prophetic events unfold before your eyes. You believed in your heart of hearts that he truly was the promised anointed one—the Messiah. You believed he was God in human flesh.

Yet in all of this excitement, you (like every other Jew) failed to realize a crucial point about the Messiah: that he was to suffer. It's not as if the Scriptures didn't speak of such things. But it was too easy to fixate on the many victorious aspects of this anointed figure rather than the more embarrassing details. Seriously, which sort of prophetic passages would you rather focus on if you were an oppressed Hebrew living in a Roman occupied land?

> You shall break them with a rod of iron and dash them in pieces like a potter's vessel.[69]

---

[69] See Psalm 2:9.

Or

> I am a worm and not a man, scorned by mankind and despised by the people.[70]

If you were a Jew living in a land in which a powerful military force controlled your everyday life and forced you to pay unrealistic sums of taxes, which sort of Messiah would you want? I think I would want to see the military hero, not a suffering servant. (By the way, both of these verses are about Jesus.)

This is where the disciples were coming from too. Sure, they heard Jesus teach about faith over and over again as they approached Jerusalem. They heard him teach about love, grace, and forgiveness. They knew about the parable of the Good Samaritan and how Jesus healed the Roman centurion's son. But as they approached Jerusalem, in the back of their minds, they were thinking that the time to rebel against the Romans had come. They had a secret weapon: Jesus. The disciples must have thought, *If he can walk on water, then surely he can command a battlefield. If Jesus can make the lame walk, then surely he can make enemy soldiers lame. If he can raise the dead, then surely he can strike down the living.* Many were convinced Jesus was a military and political leader and that he would go into Jerusalem to make war against the unjust heathen Romans.

So you can imagine their surprise when instead he said, "Hey, guys, the time has come for prophecy to be fulfilled. I am going to be handed over to the Romans. They will mock me, beat me up, and spit on me. Then they will whip me half to death and nail me to a cross."[71] The disciples would have been beside themselves. They must

---

[70] See Psalm 22:6.
[71] My paraphrase of Luke 18:31–34.

have said, "What? Not on my watch!" At a different point, Peter does protest.[72] What a deflating prediction. Talk about a buzzkill. Could Jesus be any more depressing? I bet someone had to be thinking, "I spent nearly four years following this guy all over the countryside, risking my life, and I'm not about to let him go and get himself killed." Maybe Judas thought the same way. I'm not defending the guy's actions, but it's not hard to imagine the disillusionment these words from Jesus brought upon the Twelve.

Why Jesus Predicted His Death

While Jesus knew they could not understand what he said, it was important for him to say it. For one, he used the statement to show that his death and suffering at the hands of the religious leaders and Romans did not catch him off guard. The crucifixion was not something that just happened to him beyond his control. Instead, Jesus was a willing victim. Had he wanted to avoid his fate, he would have stayed as far away from Jerusalem as possible. Instead, he faithfully carried out the Father's will, traveling up to Jerusalem even though it would result in torture.

Similarly, Jesus detailed his death and resurrection in order to demonstrate his trustworthiness. As he later said to his disciples about his betrayal, "I am telling you this now, before it takes place, that when it does take place you may believe that I am he" (John 13:19). Jesus made several similar statements regarding future events.[73] Although they could not understand what Jesus was talking about, after the fact, everything clicked into place in their minds. Who but the Son of God could predict and fulfill such events? As we know,

---

[72] See Matthew 16:21–23.
[73] See John 8:28, John 14:29, John 16:4.

God is completely trustworthy. Were he not trustworthy, he would not be God. Jesus's prediction and fulfillment of his mission at Calvary proved he was who he said he was: the Son of Man, God's representative on earth, the Christ.

This served to embolden the disciples in their faith. After seeing the resurrected Lord, they finally understood the cross was part of Jesus's plan from the beginning. *The Lord's prophecy about himself paired with all of the miracles he performed, and the lessons he gave on the road to Jerusalem prepared the disciples to live radical lives for God after Jesus ascended into heaven.* While the Gospels often depict the Twelve as flabbergasted, petty, and clueless, the resurrection and the gift of the Holy Spirit at Pentecost transformed them into pillars of faith. And they would need every ounce of faith they could muster. As they carried out Jesus's final instructions to testify to his glory throughout the world, tradition tells us all but one disciple would die as a martyr for the sake of the gospel. Of those, Andrew, Peter, Philip, Bartholomew, Thaddeus, and Simon the Zealot were crucified.[74] Had Jesus not first been crucified and resurrected, could these disciples have endured the same torture?

A Divine Foreshadow

Almost two millennia before Jesus ascended the hill called Calvary, another man climbed a hill to serve as a sacrifice. Just like Jesus, he was sentenced to death but found life three days later. Like Jesus, he bore the wooden instrument of death upon his back with the weapon in tow. He agonized up the hill that Yahweh, the one true God, chose in order to give his life at the command of his father. And as crazy as

---

[74] The facts concerning the deaths of many of the apostles are unclear. For example, some legends hold Bartholomew was beheaded while others say he was crucified upside down.

it sounds, he willingly went along with his father's instruction. At first, the circumstances of the pending sacrifice confused the son. He wondered about the lack of animal that would normally accompany them. On this day, there was no lamb.

The son pondered these things for three days as they traveled but didn't dare question his father about it. After all, it was customary for a father and son to offer a burnt offering together to the Lord on behalf of the family. Other than the absence of a lamb, nothing was out of order. Yet at last, curiosity and nervousness overcame him. "Where's the lamb?" he asked.

"God will provide the lamb."

Abraham confirmed Isaac's suspicion. There was no lamb. He was the sacrifice. But the two proceeded up the hill, the father trusting in God and Isaac trusting his father. At the summit, Abraham bound his son, and Isaac submitted to the fetters. Had he not submitted, he could have fled. Abraham had walked the earth for 130 years, while Isaac was barely thirty. And lying there on the pile of wood that he himself had carried up the hill, he held his breath as his dad unsheathed a razor-sharp flint knife. This was it for young Isaac. The moment had arrived.

None of this made sense. God had miraculously provided the son to Abraham and Sarah. They had tried to conceive in their younger years with no success. They had pleaded with the gods for a son until they finally resigned themselves to die without an heir. Abram and Sarai had assumed they were cursed. But Yahweh called out to this man and gave him an amazing promise. In his old age, he would have a son with his wife after all. The old couple had hope again.

But despite the promise, they would still have to wait decades and endure many trials before the promise came to pass. And now, thirty years after God's faithful fulfillment in the form of Isaac, Yahweh wanted Abraham to offer his son as a burnt offering?

Abraham studied the knife, running his thumbnail along the edge of the blade to check for nicks. Any imperfection might result in an imprecise cut and therefore prolonged suffering for his precious son. But the knife was clean. It seemed sharper than ever.

So Abraham raised the blade above his trembling son. He noticed that his hand, too, was quivering. He studied the neck of Isaac. One swift cut across the throat would sever the jugular and trachea, and Isaac would pass out instantaneously. He closed his eyes for a moment and strengthened his resolve. His God had given him a son; he could take him away. Opening his eyes, he looked down at his frightened son for the last time. He fixed his eyes on the incision point. If Isaac were going to attempt an escape, this was his last chance. But he didn't try to save himself. Instead, he submitted, a willful participant.

Abraham went to work, lowering the knife to his son.

"Abraham! Abraham!" a voice from heaven rang through the air.

"Here I am."

"Do not lay your hand on the boy or do anything to him, for now I know that you fear God, seeing you have not withheld your son, your only son, from me."[75]

And as Abraham looked up from his son, he saw a ram caught in a thicket nearby. The Lord had indeed provided.

I can imagine all of heaven holding its breath and watching as Abraham nearly sacrificed his son at God's command. I can imagine the Godhead expressing somehow, "This is what it will be like. This is how difficult it will be." You see, in some measure, God was rehearsing. Yes, the binding of Isaac was meant to test Abraham's faith, but on another level, it was a foreshadow of the ultimate sacrifice that was coming.

---

[75] See Genesis 22:12.

The Ultimate Act of Faith

Abraham demonstrated unbelievable faith in leading Isaac up that hill. But as incredible as it was, it pales in comparison to what happened on a nearby hill called Calvary. On the eve of his crucifixion, Jesus—in perhaps his most human moment—asked if the cup might pass. God told him there was no other way to accomplish what he had set out to do. Jesus, though fully God, was also fully human, and that human side of him had to trust in his Father. He had to have faith that God's will was the best way. That he would assist Jesus through the trial he was about to endure. This is where the rubber met the road for Jesus. He had survived temptation from the devil, tests from scholars, attempted stonings, gale-force winds. But these things were mere nicks in comparison to the gruesome torture he was about to endure.

And, I think, deep down, even though Jesus prayed for the cup to pass, he knew there was no other way. His entire life had built up to this point. He predicted his death to the disciples here on the road to Jerusalem. He had studied the prophets, what Isaiah had to say about the suffering servant who would save the people from their sins. He knew all of these things. But knowledge isn't enough. As author Frank Viola wrote, "Faith isn't something mental. It's not hope, hype, wishful thinking, or natural expectation. Faith is a specific kind of trust in God that's built on an internal knowing." The crucifixion was the ultimate act of faith, and Jesus had to trust in God to help him through the ordeal. He had to trust that this was the best thing, the best way. Jesus was only able to submit to the cross because of his intimate relationship with the Father.

The most amazing thing about the crucifixion is that Jesus could have ended it at any moment. As he said, "Do you think that I cannot appeal to my Father, and he will at once send me more than twelve legions of angels?" (Matt. 26:53). When the soldiers came to arrest him, he could have slipped away as he did when the mob tried to run him off a cliff in Luke 4. When the Romans blindfolded Jesus and struck him on the head, he knew not only who hit him but also every sin his assaulter had ever committed, and he could have cast him into hell in that very instant. When they tied him to a pole and scourged him with the flagrum, a Roman whip designed to rip flesh from its victims' backsides, he could have melted the bonds and turned the whip on the Romans as he did to the money changers in the temple courts. When Pilate interrogated the Lord, Jesus could have refuted every charge against him as he had refuted the Pharisees countless times over the previous three years. And when the rulers and soldiers shouted to him on the cross, "Save yourself!" he could have dislodged his feet and hands and restored his body as he had done for Bartimaeus, lepers, and the lame. He could have stopped the bleeding as he had stopped it for the woman who dared touch his cloak.

He could have ended the agony, the torture, the suffocation at any point from his arrest at Gethsemane to the spear thrust in his side, just as easily as we would pull our hand away from a hot stove. He could have stopped the suffering.

But he didn't.

When the soldiers arrived at Gethsemane, he submitted to the will of the Father who placed the wood on his back as he ascended the hill for the sacrifice. And, finally, the words of Abraham came to pass: the Lord will provide. God provided for us an unblemished lamb to take on our sins and die the sort of brutal, unbearable death we deserved.

For Jesus, that took faith.

The Resurrection Paved the Way

Maybe breaking the four-minute barrier was inevitable once World War II ended. Had Roger Bannister failed on that breezy May day at Oxford, maybe John Landy still would have ran the mile in 3:57.9 on June 21, 1954. We can't know for sure, but one thing I do know: anyone who, on May 5, 1954, doubted the possibility of sub-four-minute miles became a believer on May 6. And the collective faith of sports fans and competitors alike at witnessing the impossible paved the way for runners to break the four-minute barrier hundreds of times more.

In a more perfect way, the passion of Christ and his subsequent resurrection on the third day paved the way for you and me to embrace faith—just as those actions emboldened the disciples to live lives of faith. Do you think they would have allowed themselves to be martyred if they didn't see the resurrected Lord? If it were all some big hoax, would they have persisted in face of persecution? The same principle applies to us. Few of us will have to face martyrdom, but God is calling us daily to walk in faith, to live in step with the Spirit, to do something uncomfortable for the sake of the kingdom. The resurrection makes this all possible, just as Roger Bannister paved a trail for middle-distance runners all over the world.

Jesus demonstrated the most extreme faith the world has ever known by placing his trust in the Father and submitting to the cross. Jesus took that cup of bitterness and drank every last drop, and, in so doing, changed the destiny of mankind. Were it not for the obedience of Christ and his resurrection, faith of any measure would be impossible.

But with such extreme examples in Jesus and later in his disciples, you might be feeling overwhelmed. You might be thinking, *I could never do anything like that.* Maybe God's not asking you to. In an earlier parable, Jesus said, "One who is faithful in a very little is also faithful in much" (Luke 16:10). Maybe God's waiting for you to demonstrate faith in the little things before he will entrust you with bigger tasks. Maybe it's something as simple as knocking on your neighbor's door and inviting him to church. Perhaps God's asking you to read the Bible to your children once a week. Maybe he wants you to devote 10 percent of your income to the church. These things seem so basic. They seem ineffectual. Boring. Insignificant. How could we possibly advance God's kingdom with such muted efforts?

Don't underestimate the effectiveness of a little faith. Jesus said faith is like a mustard seed, the tiniest of seeds, that yields an enormous tree. Only God can make that happen, but it starts with you. You must place your trust in him.

I'm not saying God will never ask you to do something major like move to another city, give up a lucrative career for ministry, submit yourself to persecution, or risk being ostracized from your own family. That very well could happen. But I think that many times, God wants us to express faith in the little things, the mundane things, the mustard seed things before he will task us with the more daring steps of faith. If you're reading this book, and you've made it all the way to this last lesson, I have no doubt you have a heart for the Lord and want to do great things for his kingdom. But we must trust in God for his timing, and not force the issue. Think of Jesus high atop the temple where Satan tempted him to jump off and rely on the angels to catch him. Doing so would have revealed himself as the Messiah to the Jewish people before his hour had come. Jesus would have been forcing the issue rather than patiently carrying out God's will for three years. Rather than testing God, allow him to test you that when your hour does come, you may faithfully drink the cup the Lord has placed before you. These moments of ordinary faith, like the miniscule mustard seed, can lead to extraordinary outcomes.

But even ordinary faith takes courage. In fact, there's something very unordinary about ordinary faith. I'm sure you've seen the silly team-building exercise known as the trust fall. This is where a group divides into pairs and one, with her back to the other, leans and falls into the arms of her partner. As silly as the exercise is, it nevertheless drives home an important point. Even that small act of falling backward is scary. It requires faith. We must succumb to gravity without knowing the outcome of our fall. Even though we know the partner is mere inches away ready to catch, something inside of us shouts, *Don't do that! You will get hurt!* If we struggle to have faith in even these most trivial moments, how then can we express faith in the big things? Again, it goes back to the cross. Jesus predicted his death and resurrection and then fulfilled it. In doing so, he demonstrated his trustworthiness. No doubt you know these things, but head knowledge can only carry you so far. The Spirit will guide you, but at some point, you must take a step of faith. As author John Ortberg wrote, "You will never know God is trustworthy if you don't risk obeying him."[76] Fear is kind of like manure: it stinks, but it provides the best opportunity for growth. Each time we face fear, God uses it to increase our faith. So why not allow him to demonstrate his trustworthiness in your own life?

This is not to claim you will never get hurt, become sad, or be betrayed. Sometimes we will get hurt. After all, Jesus gave everything for us. But, when your actions are driven by faith, God will use them to advance the kingdom and, ultimately, for your benefit. As Paul wrote, "For those who love God all things work together for good" (Rom. 8:28). Every human on earth—believer or not—faces trials, pain, and suffering. We live in a fallen world, and no one is immune to the consequences of the sin of Adam and Eve. Nevertheless, when

---

[76] Ortberg, 230.

centered in God's will, your suffering can have a purpose. It can be a source of good for those around you. So you want to change the world? You want to do grandiose things for God? *Take baby steps of faith.* Risk obeying your heavenly Father. In this way, the ordinary will become extraordinary.

Just as Jesus predicted his death and resurrection, he also said he is coming again. In his absence, may we engage in our Father's business in anticipation of that day. James tells us this life is like a vapor, here one moment and gone in the next.[77] God is calling you to a life of faith. He wants to use you where you are to be his hands and feet on earth. So why delay? When it seems like darkness is winning, the only solution is to carry the light of Christ with you and trust in him to guide your every step. Andrew and I cannot tell you exactly what those steps are, but the Spirit can. And as you lean on him for guidance, your light will shine brighter for those in darkness to see.

---

[77] See James 4:14.

Don't forget your free gift!
The 39 Parables of Christ, Explained

Don't forget to download your free quick reference guide to the parables of Jesus.

You'll get a nifty PDF in an easy-to-read format listing and briefly explaining all 39 parables recorded in the Bible.

Visit bit.ly/39Parables to download your free guide.

Acknowledgments

Daniel would like to acknowledge Calvary Church for their continued encouragement as this book was being written. The church has been nothing but supportive in the pursuit of taking the Gospel across the street and across the world!

Andrew would like to acknowledge his family for their understanding and patience throughout the process of writing this book, and Kendall Davis for helping transform a rough collocation of words into something more cogent.

About the Authors

Daniel Sweet is the pastor of Calvary Free Will Baptist Church in Norman, Oklahoma. He is a graduate of Randall University in Moore, Oklahoma, and earned an MDiv from Liberty Baptist Theological Seminary. He and his wife, Jamie, of sixteen years have a heart for adoption. Of their four children, they adopted one from Vietnam and another from Tulsa. His full testimony can be seen on his website at truthneverdies.tv.

Andrew Gilmore writes for people who crave a deeper relationship with God but might not know where to begin. His aim is to inspire readers to live by faith by tugging at their heartstrings one moment and making them laugh out loud in the next. When he's not writing, you can find him eating way too much barbecue, wrestling with his kids, or watching really bad movies. He and his wife Katie live in Norman, Oklahoma with their four children. Learn more about Andrew at bit.ly/about-andrew.

Connect with the Authors

Andrew:
Twitter: @theAndyGilmore
Facebook: facebook.com/andrewgilmorenet

Daniel:
Twitter: @pastor_sweet
Facebook: facebook.com/calvarychurchnorman/

www.ingramcontent.com/pod-product-compliance
Lightning Source LLC
Chambersburg PA
CBHW021951290426
44108CB00012B/1030